Teaching Transnational Youth

Literacy and Education in a Changing World

Allison Skerrett

Foreword by
Randy Bomer

TEACHERS COLLEGE PRESS
TEACHERS COLLEGE | COLUMBIA UNIVERSITY
NEW YORK AND LONDON

Published by Teachers College Press, 1234 Amsterdam Avenue, New York, NY 10027

The author would like to express gratitude for permission to use the following:

Skerrett, A. (2011). A case of generativity in a culturally and linguistically complex English language arts classroom. *Changing English: Studies in Culture and Education, 18*(1), 85–97. Copyright Taylor and Francis Group (tandfonline.com).

Skerrett, A. (2012). Languages and literacies in translocation: Experiences and perspectives of a transnational youth. *Journal of Literacy Research, 44*(4), 364–395. Copyright SAGE Publications.

Skerrett, A. (2013). Building multiliterate and multilingual writing practices and identities. *English Education, 45*(4), 322–360. Copyright National Council of Teachers of English (NCTE).

Skerrett, A. (in press). "Closer to God": Following religion across the lifeworlds of an urban youth. *Urban Education.* DOI: 10.1177/0042085914549365.

Skerrett, A., & Bomer, R. (2011.) Borderzones in adolescents' literacy practices: Connecting out-of-school literacies to the reading curriculum. *Urban Education, 46*(6), 1256–1279. Copyright SAGE Publications.

Skerrett, A., & Bomer, R. (2013). Recruiting languages and lifeworlds for border-crossing compositions. *Research in the Teaching of English, 47*(3), 313–337. Copyright National Council of Teachers of English (NCTE).

Skerrett, A., Fowler-Amato, M., Chamberlain, K., & Sharp, C. (2012). Writing across lifeworlds. In P. J. Dunston & S. K. Fullerton (Eds.), *61st Yearbook of the Literacy Research Association* (pp. 132–144). Oak Creek, WI: Literacy Research Association, Inc. Copyright Literacy Research Association.

Library of Congress Cataloging-in-Publication Data is available at loc.gov

ISBN 978-0-8077-5658-4 (paper)
ISBN 978-0-8077-5659-1 (hardcover)
ISBN 978-0-8077-7381-9 (ebook)

Printed on acid-free paper
Manufactured in the United States of America

22 21 20 19 18 17 16 15   8 7 6 5 4 3 2 1

LANGUAGE AND LITERACY SERIES

Teaching Transnational Youth—
Literacy and Education in a Changing World
ALLISON SKERRETT

Uncommonly Good Ideas—
Teaching Writing in the Common Core Era
SANDRA MURPHY & MARY ANN SMITH

The One-on-One Reading and Writing Conference:
Working with Students on Complex Texts
JENNIFER BERNE & SOPHIE C. DEGENER

Critical Encounters in Secondary English:
Teaching Literary Theory to Adolescents, Third Edition
DEBORAH APPLEMAN

Transforming Talk into Text—
Argument Writing, Inquiry, and Discussion, Grade 6–12
THOMAS M. MCCANN

Reading and Representing Across the Content Areas:
A Classroom Guide
AMY ALEXANDRA WILSON & KATHRYN J. CHAVEZ

Writing and Teaching to Change the World:
Connecting with Our Most Vulnerable Students
STEPHANIE JONES, ED.

Educating Literacy Teachers Online:
Tools, Techniques, and Transformations
LANE W. CLARKE & SUSAN WATTS-TAFFE

Other People's English: Code-Meshing, Code-Switching, and African American Literacy
VERSHAWN ASHANTI YOUNG, RUSTY BARRETT, Y'SHANDA YOUNG-RIVERA, & KIM BRIAN LOVEJOY

WHAM! Teaching with Graphic Novels Across the Curriculum
WILLIAM G. BROZO, GARY MOORMAN, & CARLA K. MEYER

The Administration and Supervision of Reading Programs, 5th Edition
SHELLEY B. WEPNER, DOROTHY S. STRICKLAND, & DIANA J. QUATROCHE, EDS.

Critical Literacy in the Early Childhood Classroom:
Unpacking Histories, Unlearning Privilege
CANDACE R. KUBY

Inspiring Dialogue:
Talking to Learn in the English Classroom
MARY M. JUZWIK, CARLIN BORSHEIM-BLACK, SAMANTHA CAUGHLAN, & ANNE HEINTZ

Reading the Visual:
An Introduction to Teaching Multimodal Literacy
FRANK SERAFINI

Race, Community, and Urban Schools:
Partnering with African American Families
STUART GREENE

ReWRITING the Basics:
Literacy Learning in Children's Cultures
ANNE HAAS DYSON

Writing Instruction That Works:
Proven Methods for Middle and High School Classrooms
ARTHUR N. APPLEBEE & JUDITH A. LANGER, WITH KRISTEN CAMPBELL WILCOX, MARC NACHOWITZ, MICHAEL P. MASTROIANNI, AND CHRISTINE DAWSON

Literacy Playshop: New Literacies, Popular Media, and Play in the Early Childhood Classroom
KAREN E. WOHLWEND

Critical Media Pedagogy:
Teaching for Achievement in City Schools
ERNEST MORRELL, RUDY DUEÑAS, VERONICA GARCIA, & JORGE LOPEZ

A Search Past Silence:
The Literacy of Young Black Men
DAVID E. KIRKLAND

The ELL Writer:
Moving Beyond Basics in the Secondary Classroom
CHRISTINA ORTMEIER-HOOPER

Reading in a Participatory Culture:
Remixing *Moby-Dick* in the English Classroom
HENRY JENKINS & WYN KELLEY, WITH KATIE CLINTON, JENNA MCWILLIAMS, RICARDO PITTS-WILEY, AND ERIN REILLY, EDS.

Summer Reading: Closing the Rich/Poor Achievement Gap
RICHARD L. ALLINGTON & ANNE MCGILL-FRANZEN, EDS.

Real World Writing for Secondary Students:
Teaching the College Admission Essay and Other Gate-Openers for Higher Education
JESSICA SINGER EARLY & MEREDITH DECOSTA

Teaching Vocabulary to English Language Learners
MICHAEL F. GRAVES, DIANE AUGUST, & JEANNETTE MANCILLA-MARTINEZ

Literacy for a Better World:
The Promise of Teaching in Diverse Schools
LAURA SCHNEIDER VANDERPLOEG

Socially Responsible Literacy:
Teaching Adolescents for Purpose and Power
PAULA M. SELVESTER & DEBORAH G. SUMMERS

Learning from Culturally and Linguistically Diverse Classrooms: Using Inquiry to Inform Practice
JOAN C. FINGON & SHARON H. ULANOFF, EDS.

Bridging Literacy and Equity
ALTHIER M. LAZAR, PATRICIA A. EDWARDS, & GWENDOLYN THOMPSON MCMILLON

"Trust Me! I Can Read"
SALLY LAMPING & DEAN WOODRING BLASE

Reading Girls
HADAR DUBOWSKY MA'AYAN

Reading Time
CATHERINE COMPTON-LILLY

A Call to Creativity
LUKE REYNOLDS

(continued)

For volumes in the NCRLL Collection (edited by JoBeth Allen and Donna E. Alvermann) and the Practitioners Bookshelf Series (edited by Celia Genishi and Donna E. Alvermann), as well as a complete list of titles in this series, please visit www.tcpress.com.

Literacy and Justice Through Photography
WENDY EWALD, KATHERINE HYDE, & LISA LORD

The Successful High School Writing Center
DAWN FELS & JENNIFER WELLS, EDS.

Interrupting Hate
MOLLIE V. BLACKBURN

Playing Their Way into Literacies
KAREN E. WOHLWEND

Teaching Literacy for Love and Wisdom
JEFFREY D. WILHELM & BRUCE NOVAK

Overtested
JESSICA ZACHER PANDYA

Restructuring Schools for Linguistic Diversity, Second Edition
OFELIA B. MIRAMONTES, ADEL NADEAU, & NANCY L. COMMINS

Words Were All We Had
MARÍA DE LA LUZ REYES, ED.

Urban Literacies
VALERIE KINLOCH, ED.

Bedtime Stories and Book Reports
CATHERINE COMPTON-LILLY & STUART GREENE, EDS.

Envisioning Knowledge
JUDITH A. LANGER

Envisioning Literature, Second Edition
JUDITH A. LANGER

Writing Assessment and the Revolution in Digital Texts and Technologies
MICHAEL R. NEAL

Artifactual Literacies
KATE PAHL & JENNIFER ROWSELL

Educating Emergent Bilinguals
OFELIA GARCÍA & JO ANNE KLEIFGEN

(Re)Imagining Content-Area Literacy Instruction
RONI JO DRAPER, ED.

Change Is Gonna Come
PATRICIA A. EDWARDS, GWENDOLYN THOMPSON MCMILLON, & JENNIFER D. TURNER

When Commas Meet Kryptonite
MICHAEL BITZ

Literacy Tools in the Classroom
RICHARD BEACH, GERALD CAMPANO, BRIAN EDMISTON, & MELISSA BORGMANN

Harlem on Our Minds
VALERIE KINLOCH

Teaching the New Writing
ANNE HERRINGTON, KEVIN HODGSON, & CHARLES MORAN, EDS.

Children, Language, and Literacy
CELIA GENISHI & ANNE HAAS DYSON

Children's Language
JUDITH WELLS LINDFORS

"You Gotta BE the Book," Second Edition
JEFFREY D. WILHELM

No Quick Fix
RICHARD L. ALLINGTON & SEAN A. WALMSLEY, EDS.

Children's Literature and Learning
BARBARA A. LEHMAN

Storytime
LARWRENCE R. SIPE

Effective Instruction for Struggling Readers, K–6
BARBARA M. TAYLOR & JAMES E. YSSELDYKE, EDS.

The Effective Literacy Coach
ADRIAN RODGERS & EMILY M. RODGERS

Writing in Rhythm
MAISHA T. FISHER

Reading the Media
RENEE HOBBS

teaching**media***literacy*.com
RICHARD BEACH

What Was It Like?
LINDA J. RICE

Research on Composition
PETER SMAGORINSKY, ED.

The Vocabulary Book
MICHAEL F. GRAVES

Powerful Magic
NINA MIKKELSEN

New Literacies in Action
WILLIAM KIST

Teaching English Today
BARRIE R.C. BARRELL ET AL., EDS.

Bridging the Literacy Achievement Gap, 4–12
DOROTHY S. STRICKLAND & DONNA E. ALVERMANN, EDS.

Out of This World
HOLLY VIRGINIA BLACKFORD

Critical Passages
KRISTIN DOMBEK & SCOTT HERNDON

Making Race Visible
STUART GREENE & DAWN ABT-PERKINS, EDS.

The Child as Critic, Fourth Edition
GLENNA SLOAN

Room for Talk
REBEKAH FASSLER

Give Them Poetry!
GLENNA SLOAN

The Brothers and Sisters Learn to Write
ANNE HAAS DYSON

"Just Playing the Part"
CHRISTOPHER WORTHMAN

The Testing Trap
GEORGE HILLOCKS, JR.

Inquiry Into Meaning
EDWARD CHITTENDEN & TERRY SALINGER, WITH ANNE M. BUSSIS

"Why Don't They Learn English?"
LUCY TSE

Conversational Borderlands
BETSY RYMES

Inquiry-Based English Instruction
RICHARD BEACH & JAMIE MYERS

For my parents, Theresa and James Skerrett.
Thank you for your love, wisdom, courage,
and sacrifice in shaping us into a transnational family.

Contents

Foreword

Allison Skerrett asks us to think more carefully about borders. She pushes us to reconsider a collection of different ones—borders between countries, of course, but also those that divide school from the rest of life, that divide disciplines and school subjects, and that divide the successful from the struggling students.

As she explains in this book, we might be accustomed to thinking of young people who arrive in our school from another country as immigrants—people who crossed a border once and for all, permanently moving from another nation state to the United States. But for many students, technological and trade changes, such as relatively inexpensive travel and the expansion of Internet access, have made it more likely that they repeatedly crisscross borders over large chunks of their lives. Living in more than one country means that an educational goal of "assimilation" or "Americanization" so common in the early 20th century is quite impractical and not a legitimate goal.

Dr. Skerrett suggests in this book that we educate students to draw on *their own diversity*—the resources and flexibilities they have earned through their crossing of all kinds of borders in their lives. So, teaching literacy goes beyond a teacher setting up an environment with institutionally valued forms of literacy available for students to internalize. Instead, teaching literacy also involves pointing students toward noticing, valuing, and capitalizing upon literate practices that are outside our control—practices they got someplace else. That means teachers have to be open and flexible, noticing and entertaining different types of literacy—i.e., ranges of actions people commit with text—ideas not their own and, moreover, not sanctioned by the official curriculum documents that increasingly seek to control and constrain teaching.

Opening a curriculum so that it builds upon the wealth of resources that transnational students bring to school requires a change in the way educators think about students whose lives include such large and significant movement. Most groups have always regarded outsiders as the Other, as less-than, as dangerous. This negative regard is a logical extension of the impulses that draws borders around nations in the first place. In the United States, there is a strong tradition of seeing newcomers as unwashed hordes—as tired, poor, huddled, yearning masses, as wretched refuse. Those last words are, of course, from Emma Lazarus's poem "The New Colossus," associated with the Statue of Liberty, and that poem does have the substantial virtue of at least being kind toward people from other countries who want to move to the United States, in sharp contrast to much of today's nativist paranoia and hatefulness. In many contemporary conversations about transnational individuals, calling people wretched refuse is an unusually nice thing to say. But it actually matters—politically, socially, ethically, and educationally—how people regard one another, and it matters, in particular, how teachers regard their students.

South African educator Hilary Janks once said to me, "where there is difference, there will be stratification." People know their own groups and assign value to other groups as "higher than ours" or "lower than ours." In a country like the United States, it is not unusual for people from other nations to be identified as a group at a lower level than individuals born here. That's not justifiable, but it's not surprising, especially since, as a group, those from other countries are being defined for what they are not: U.S. natives. That is deficit thinking by nature: regarding people in terms of what they are not, rather than what they are. This deficit thinking also serves as a cover story, legitimating stratification, oppression, and a curriculum that does not recognize difference.

Schools have a history of regarding difference as a problem, and one form of this negative regard has been directed toward students from other lands, with their obvious cultural and linguistic differences. If they are different—really different—we look for a source of deficiency; maybe it's genetic, or inexperience, or poverty; perhaps it's something amiss in the root culture or the way their home culture makes contact with that of the contemporary United States. Even if this deficit thinking seems unavoidable in U.S. schools as institutions, Allison Skerrett shows in this book that teachers can mitigate its harm through specific choices in their teaching, by viewing difference as a resource that is available to a greater degree when we are fortunate enough to have transnational students in our classrooms.

Randy Bomer

Preface

This book comes at a time of emergent forms of student diversity in all schooling environments. While we have been hard at work teaching responsively to our culturally and linguistically diverse students, an underrecognized form of student diversity has been rapidly gaining a presence in our classrooms, propelled by the swelling global phenomenon of transnationalism. Transnational people, through a mix of necessity and choice, embark on a mobile international lifestyle to take advantage of economic, social, educational, and other opportunities across two or more nations. Researchers estimate that as many as one in four school-age youths participate in transnational life (e.g., Coe, Reynolds, Boehm, Hess, & Rae-Espinoza, 2011). What this means is that many of our classrooms, perhaps without our knowing, include students who have deep and expansive ties to other countries. Transnational lifestyles enable youths to develop unique forms of knowledge and language and literacy practices that can benefit literacy teaching and learning in our classrooms. Yet transnational life can also introduce educational challenges for our students and our teaching. Literacy researchers have recently begun to explore how young people use and develop their language and literacy practices through transnational life. As this body of scholarship slowly accumulates, literacy educators urgently need professional guidance about how, through our educational practices, we can become more aware of and responsive to the transnational students in our care.

This book is the first of its kind to provide guidance about how literacy education today can better support transnational students. Whether they are seasoned professionals or preservice teachers, literacy teacher educators, or scholars of language and literacy invested in the educational outcomes of transnational youths, all literacy/language arts teachers can learn something from this book. The book draws upon research-based approaches and the exemplary practices of literacy teachers whose classrooms include transnational students to demonstrate how attending to transnationalism in students' lives can deepen and expand the literacy teaching and learning that is already happening in diverse classrooms.

The book is organized into six chapters that progressively build an approach to foregrounding transnationalism in literacy education for the benefit of both transnational students and their mononational classmates. The introductory chapter reviews the literature on transnational youths and the research and educational theories that inform the book. Thereafter, each successive chapter explores an aspect of literacy educational practice that we can make more inclusive and supportive of transnational youths. Every chapter opens with the voices and experiences of a transnational student, an exemplary teacher of transnational students, or a classroom interaction to highlight the primary concepts being explored in that chapter. Each chapter then closes by providing explicit instructional suggestions that teachers can use to highlight or introduce the educational practices examined in the chapter in their own classrooms.

Chapter 2 explores how we can learn about all our students' knowledge, experiences, and language and literacy practices and conceptualize transnational students' repertoires within the total set of educational resources that our diverse students bring to school. Chapter 3 then takes us through sound curricular and instructional approaches in literacy classrooms—reading, writing, and critical inquiry—and shows us how we can make these teaching and learning experiences more powerful by investing them with the transnational resources, along with the other diverse learning repertoires, we have discovered among our students.

Chapters 4 and 5 foreground transnational students' movements across different national contexts in which they may or may not enroll in formal schooling and discuss the importance of teaching with awareness of the literacy learning opportunities available to our students across transnational life. The chapters offer a variety of strategies through which we can stay abreast of, and provide support to, our transnational students' literacy learning in other countries, whether these happen in school or nonschool contexts. The chapters also provide approaches through which we can enlist the support of other stakeholders who are invested in our transnational students' education, and equip our students themselves to take ownership of their literacy development within and outside of school contexts. Furthermore, I explain how the ideas in these chapters have direct relevance for teachers who want to sponsor the literacy development of all students, regardless of their transnational status, as people who participate in many formal and informal contexts of literacy practice outside our classrooms.

I wrap up the book by framing teaching with awareness of transnationalism as a socially just and equity-minded educational response given the growing numbers of transnational students in schools today. I further highlight unique and important outcomes and gains that all our students will accomplish from engaging with transnationalism in literacy education. These achievements, which are essential for all people in an increasingly globalized world, include in-depth world knowledge, a sense of global citizenship, and cultural and linguistic flexibility. Foremost for our work as literacy educators, all of our students will develop stronger as well as more specialized abilities to read, write, investigate, analyze, interact, think, know, and act in ways that are deeply and critically informed by a transnational standpoint. I hope literacy educators, scholars, and others who read this book will be compelled by its educational urgency and relevance, theoretical and research bases, and explicit instructional guidance into making our educational practices more responsive to the accelerating populations of transnational youths across our schools in this continuously changing world.

Acknowledgments

This book has emerged from a long and diverse line of people, experiences, and opportunities that God has orchestrated as my life and I wish to recognize and thank Him and other highly significant people who have helped me bring this work to fruition. My husband, Peter, and the joy of our lives, Peter Pie, thank you for valuing the work that is important to me while reminding me each evening that our time together is what is most meaningful about each day, and in life. To our immediate families in Boston, thanks for accepting the 2,000 miles that physically separate us and loving us generously across them.

Beyond my family, I belong to the most brilliant, caring, collegial, and fun community of literacy scholars (both students and faculty) at The University of Texas at Austin. To my colleagues Randy Bomer, Nancy Roser, Jim Hoffman, Jo Worthy, Beth Maloch, Melissa Wetzel, Ramon Martinez, and Deb Kelt, thank you so much for your friendship and professional support. Here, I must especially thank Randy Bomer and Nancy Roser. Nancy continues to be a flawless example for me of what it means to be a caring and supportive colleague and friend. Randy has also been my unwavering supporter, but most importantly, my mentor and teacher throughout my 8 years at UT. Anyone who knows Randy's work and reads this book will recognize that I owe a large part of my learning and thinking about young people and their literate lives to his teaching and mentorship.

In a related vein, I must also say a very special thank-you to Deb Kelt for allowing me into your classroom to learn from your exemplary teaching and care for all your students, and especially, in line with the theme of this work, your transnational students. I am, moreover, incredibly fortunate (and I know it was yet another orchestrated moment of my life's plan), that Emily Spangler, my editor at Teachers College Press, picked up an article I published in the *Journal of Literacy Research* that investigated the transnational life and language and literacy repertoires of a young woman I met in Deb's classroom. Emily, thank you for encouraging me to consider writing this book and for investing your substantial professional expertise in shaping this work into what it has become.

Moving in my mind back to Boston for a few moments, I also wish to recognize and thank Professor Andy Hargreaves at Boston College, who first mentored me into educational research; and to Dr. Leigh Patel, also at Boston College, who first encouraged me to seek out the voices of young people as I inquired into issues of student diversity and literacy education. In this regard, I am also deeply indebted to, and thankful for, all my former students at Dorchester High School in Boston, and more recently, youths in Austin and in the Caribbean islands of St. Martin, St. Maarten, and Dominica, who honored me by allowing me to teach them, and learn from them as well, about what constitutes a powerful and meaningful form of literacy education for diverse youths, including transnational students.

This mention of the geography of the Caribbean brings me to my core identity as an adolescent immigrant to the United States but one whose family had become transnational beginning very early in my childhood and continues to be transnational today. My parents, and in particular my mother (because I saw her experience the benefits, hurts, and uncertainties of their decision daily), were loving, wise, and sacrificial in embarking upon a transnational lifestyle that ensured all their children had opportunities to pursue their educational and other life goals. Transnational life fundamentally shifted our understandings and experiences of family, togetherness, and separation; generated new forms of literacy practice to sustain us in those borderlands; and made us into people who are willing to engage productively with and across diversity and difference, in people, in places, and within our ever-changing identities and lives. Thank you, Mammy and Daddy. All of your children—Daniel, Herman, Jeff, Lucy, Desry, Joanne, and I—owe to you this precious inheritance of transnational life.

Teaching Transnational Youth

CHAPTER 1

Introduction

Transnationalism—What It Is, How It Is Changing Societies and Schools, and Why It Should Change Literacy Education

Vanesa was 15 years old when I met her in a 9th-grade literacy classroom in which I was doing research. Vanesa had been living transnationally since the age of 12, moving between an urbanizing community in Austin, Texas, and the small town right outside of Mexico City in which she was born. In her 9th-grade year, the family's transnational living situation involved Vanesa, her mother, her younger sister, and a new baby brother, who was born in Texas, all living together in the United States. The children's father lived primarily in Mexico to run a family-owned business, but he visited them regularly for weeks at a time. During school vacations and for important events in Mexico, Vanesa's mother and the children were the ones to cross the United States–Mexico border to participate in the lives they maintained there.

Cameron was 17 years old when I met him. He was born on Dutch St. Maarten, where his parents met, but was raised in French St. Martin, where his father was from. Cameron was born into a transnational family. His mother was born on Dutch St. Maarten but she had lived and completed high school in New York City before moving back to the island. Cameron's family maintained close ties to New York—he had been visiting New York with his mother almost every year of his life. Cameron and his family had a passion for singing and playing music that spanned the transnational contexts of St. Martin, St. Maarten, and New York City. During his visits to New York, Cameron found that the music world of New York City offered grander opportunities than St. Martin for developing his talents, so he decided to complete high school at his mother's alma mater, a performing arts academy.

Seventeen-year-old Monica, like Cameron, was born in Dutch St. Maarten. Her mother immigrated to the island from Curaçao, another Dutch-speaking Caribbean island, where she met Monica's father, a native citizen

> of St. Maarten. Monica's father lived a transnational lifestyle for economic purposes; he had worked on that island as well as in Connecticut and Florida. Monica had lived with her mother in St. Maarten as a young child, and her early schooling occurred there. Since the age of 9, Monica had lived and gone to school in central Florida, where her father lived, but she spent summers and other holidays with her mother in St. Maarten. During the middle of her junior year of high school in Florida, Monica's father decided to take a new job opportunity in St. Maarten. Monica was thus suddenly returned to St. Maarten and reinstated in school there.

We live in an era of unprecedented, rapid upswings in the number of transnational youths in societies and schools across the world (Coe, Reynolds, Boehm, Hess, & Rae-Espinoza, 2011; Graham & Jordan, 2011; Hamann & Zúñiga, 2011; Hamann, Zúñiga, & Sánchez García, 2006; Mazzucato & Schans, 2011). Unlike immigrant youths, whose feet are firmly planted in their new homeland, transnational youths maintain significant ties to two or more nation-states. Consequently, they acquire experiences, understandings, networks, and deep attachments—spanning personal, familial, educational, economic, religious, and other domains—across multiple societies (Bernardi, 2011; Hershberg & Lykes, 2013; Nobles, 2011; Sánchez, 2007a, 2009; Zúñiga & Hamann, 2009). In response to the growing incidence of transnational youths, literacy scholars have begun to explore how young people experience transnational life, and, in particular, how their language and literacy practices shape, and are shaped by, their transnational circumstances (Araujo & de la Piedra, 2013; Jiménez, Smith, & Teague, 2009; Lam & Rosario-Ramos, 2009; Lam & Warriner, 2012; Sánchez, 2007a, 2007b, 2009; Skerrett, 2012a, 2013; Skerrett & Bomer, 2013). However, literacy scholars have yet to inquire into, theorize, and develop approaches to literacy education that can support the academic development of transnational youths across the countries (and regions within national geographies) in which they are schooled. In this book, I examine the phenomenon of transnational life as experienced by diverse adolescents who live and go to school across a range of national contexts—major cities in the United States and Canada, some regions of Mexico, and the Caribbean islands of Dominica, Dutch St. Maarten, and French St. Martin. I draw from these youths' and their teachers' experiences of, and perspectives on, language, literacy, and educational practices across transnational life to develop approaches to literacy education that are aware, supportive, and inclusive of transnational youths.

WHO ARE TRANSNATIONAL YOUTHS? WHAT DOES RESEARCH SAY ABOUT THEIR LIVES?

Researchers estimate that one in four children, totaling several million worldwide, lead transnational lives across diverse world nations in Africa, the Americas, Asia, and Europe (Graham & Jordan, 2011; Mazzucato & Schans, 2011). Although there are no official statistics on the numbers of transnational families and youths in nations such as the United States, researchers investigating transnational populations claim that there are anywhere from hundreds of thousands (Coe et al., 2011; Zúñiga & Hamann, 2009) to millions (Graham & Jordan, 2011) of transnational students in schools at any given point. This lack of specifics about the numbers of youths living transnationally reflects educational policymakers' and researchers' limited attention to this circumstance (Mazzucato & Schans, 2011). Another difficulty in identifying the number of transnational students in schools lies in the miscategorization of these youths as immigrant students (Zúñiga & Hamann, 2009). Recent U.S. Census statistics, for example, that show a rise in immigrant students in urban schools (National Center for Educational Statistics, 2013) suggest that there are greater numbers of transnational youths in schools than educators may imagine. Too often, schools learn that some of their students are transnational, rather than immigrant, after these students disappear for a lengthy period of time only to return unexpectedly. Sometimes, the transnational youths return to a different state or region of a country from the one they departed and thus their new schools and teachers may consider them recently arrived immigrants when, in fact, the young people have prior educational knowledge and experiences with schools in that country.

Children and youths frequently embark on a transnational lifestyle because their parents or other relatives choose a mobile international lifestyle to take advantage of economic, social, and educational opportunities across two or more nations (Bernardi, 2011; Bledsoe & Sow, 2011; Hershberg & Lykes, 2013; Nobles, 2011; Sánchez, 2007a, 2007b, 2009; Zúñiga & Hamann, 2009). Vanesa, one of the transnational youths I introduced above, explained to me the economic reasons behind her family's transnational lifestyle:

> My dad has a company there in Mexico, so he's like really important so he cannot leave it there and come back with us. So, like, he comes back and forth to Texas and Mexico. Yeah, and my mom is always with me.

Sometimes, youths like Monica, whom you also met briefly above, become transnational people because parents who live in one country (I'll call it TC 1—Transnational Country 1, which functions as the original point of migration) will send them off to live with relatives or family friends in another land, TC 2 (Transnational Country 2), so they can have better educational opportunities (Bernardi, 2011; Coe et al., 2011). These youths may attend schools for much of the school year in TC 2 but leave for extended periods of time—for instance, adding several weeks or more to official school breaks so they can be with their families in TC 1. This was Monica's experience, although the sending children away scenario may not always involve frequent physical contact between the children and the families they have left in TC 1. This situation happened in my own family on the Caribbean island of Dominica where I was born. My mother had two boys from a previous relationship before she married my father, and my brothers' father had immigrated to California for better economic prospects and settled there, buying a home and getting married. The adults involved decided that the boys, who were then 9 and 11, would have better educational and overall life opportunities if they joined their father in the United States. Notwithstanding the boys' views on the situation—especially my older brother, who was emotionally distraught about being apart from his mother and sisters—they were sent to live with their father in California. Five years went by before their first return to Dominica.

In another transnational configuration, youths may become transnational when one or both of their parents migrate abroad for improved economic prospects, leaving them behind in TC 1, but arranging visits and reunions in TC 1 or TC 2. Such visits can be frequent or rare, extended or brief (Nobles, 2011). Indeed, in doing research for this book I came to the startling realization that since I was 2 (before my brothers or I and the rest of my family immigrated to the United States), my family had been living transnationally. This was because, for 13 years, my father worked as a seaman transporting goods across different Caribbean nations. This job required him to be away at sea for 6 months at a time before he would earn a mere 2 weeks at home with his family. It was only after many years of political, social, and economic resource building and strategizing that my family was able to live together as immigrants in the United States who still maintained significant ties to our homeland—deep relationships with extended family, close friends, and our church; keeping our home and visiting frequently; and participating in the economy through flows of money and goods. In short, we continued to *be* a transnational family through a different configuration of transnational life. Yet, prior to my research on transnational youths, I had identified only as an adolescent immigrant to the United States whose family remained connected to her home country, rather than as someone whose core identity and life experience had been deeply shaped by transnationalism.

Considering yet another scenario of maximizing economic opportunities transnationally, agricultural or other seasonal workers may take their children with them into a country, TC 2, where the adults will work for several months of an agricultural season. The children in these families will attend school in TC 2 for several months or more at a time. Such families establish homes, social relationships, functional and leisure activities and routines, and all the other vital ingredients that make TC 2 a real home for them. After the work season ends, the family will return to TC 1 and rekindle their home life there for a variety of reasons—because it offers a cheaper cost of living, thus allowing them to better economize the earnings they have saved; because of strong family and cultural ties; or because they do not have permanent residency status in TC 2. Their children are then reinstated in the schools in TC 1 for another period of several months. Sometimes, depending on the length of their stay, or the educational conditions in TC 1 or TC 2, the children may not enroll in formal schools. Yet the young people are involved in social life and literate activity, such as through religious or other community organizations, during their sojourns in both countries. The family then repeats this cycle of transnational mobility when a season of work presents itself in TC

2. Importantly, the family may return to a different region of TC 2, depending on agricultural and economic conditions. Thus, youths in such families may return to the same schools they originally attended or may enroll in schools in a different part of that country or region that is new to them. This last transnational scenario is a common one for families who live across countries such as the United States and Mexico that are physically proximal yet economically quite distal (Coe et al., 2011; Zúñiga & Hamann, 2009).

Even for transnational families who are less mobile across a year, unexpected or planned important events, seasons of religious and cultural observations, and other reasons may lead to transnational sojourning for varied periods of time. Vanesa shared with me how she, her mother, and siblings always returned to Mexico for Christmas and other holidays, as well as for the summer. These visits helped them sustain deep familial ties and cultural identity. As Vanesa put it: "My grandparents have like seven kids. . . . It's really nice though because [at] Christmas when we go to Mexico, oh my gosh! Our house is like full of kids running around the house. I love Christmas in Mexico."

Sometimes, transnational parents may remain in a country that they and their children entered for economic mobility and political capital, but return the children to their native countries at some point for social and cultural reasons. Bledsoe and Sow (2011), for example, documented how West African parents in Europe and North America returned their adolescent children, who were engaging in behaviors that put them at risk for racial discrimination and legal prosecution, back to West African kin. Family members in West Africa took up responsibility for resocializing the youths into African mores from which they could generate more positive attitudes and strategies to overcome social difficulties when they re-entered America or Europe. My own family dealt with this situation of socializing and nurturing children transnationally as my brothers' relationship with their father and his wife in California became strained and the boys began to have difficulties navigating the social challenges that were cropping up in the community where they lived. After months of telephone and letter communications and counseling among the adults, and between my mother and brothers (literacy practices that were produced in our family for the explicit purpose of navigating transnational life), the adults decided to return the boys to Dominica. It was 6 months before the adults deemed them better equipped to return to social life in the United States.

Families in the diverse situations I have been describing should not be understood simply as migrant workers or immigrants who spend significant amounts of time in their native countries. Rather, they are transnational people. For them, home is both here and there because of the deep and varied attachments and activities (familial, cultural, educational, and economic) they maintain in and across two or more countries (Bledsoe & Sow, 2011; Hamann et al., 2006; Nobles, 2011; Zúñiga & Hamann, 2009). Through a mixture of necessity and choice, and for varying combinations of economic, educational, political, cultural, and other exigencies, more and more youths and families are embracing or accepting a transnational life.

It is troubling, therefore, that there is limited empirical research and sparse professional knowledge and direction regarding how literacy teachers and students may engage productively with transnationalism in teaching and learning (Sánchez, 2007a, 2009; Skerrett, 2012a, 2013; Skerrett & Bomer, 2013; Zúñiga & Hamann, 2009). One outcome of this inattention is that teachers, unaware of this unique student population and their reasons for leading a transnational life, can mistakenly assume that these students and their families do not care enough about education or do not value the teaching and learning experiences that we carefully craft for our students. As an English teacher in an urban high school in Boston, I (along with my colleagues) fell into this problematic view of our transnational students, a term that was unknown to us at the time. One early conversation I had about this book was with a good friend who, like me, had been a teacher in Boston Public Schools. As I shared with my friend what I had been learning about transnational youths' circumstances of living and learning across two or more nations, she grew visibly excited at now being able to name this phenomenon that we had both experienced as urban teachers.

Throughout our years teaching in Boston, we taught students who sometimes disappeared from our classrooms for weeks or months at a time, usually without informing us of their plans to leave. From our knowledge of their backgrounds and conversations with their friends, we would surmise that they were back in the DR (Dominican Republic), Haiti, Honduras, or some other country. When they returned to us, we felt the same jolt of surprise as we had when they left. And yes, we were also, to be honest, somewhat put out that they had reappeared just as suddenly as they had vanished. It seemed to us disrespectful of our relationship and work with them as their teachers that they and their families did not inform us of their plans to leave and their intentions to return. It also seemed to impose an impossible administrative and pedagogical demand on us to reintegrate the students back into the learning community without question and with great speed. The most pressing hardship in doing this was that we had little sense of how our students had spent their time away from us, or what they learned, while they were gone. Reflecting back on those classroom experiences in light of our new knowledge about transnational youths and education, we readily discerned that our schools and our teaching had not explicitly acknowledged and invited transnational life into education.

In my current role as a secondary English teacher educator and researcher, I realize that we have still not yet fully grasped and grappled with this incidence of a growing number of transnational youths in literacy classrooms. Particularly within this overly standardized and accountability-driven educational climate, we have much to learn and consider in terms of the implications of this demographic shift for curriculum, teaching, and learning in classrooms that have long been culturally and linguistically diverse. I direct and teach in an urban English teacher preparation program at The University of Texas at Austin. The teacher candidates I prepare for teaching diverse learners arrive in urban classrooms eager to learn how teachers and students are drawing on students' cultures and existing language and literacy practices in teaching and learning academic literacies and are also excited to try out some of the instructional approaches they are learning in their university classes. The preservice teachers quickly become discouraged by what they come to learn is urban schooling in far too many contexts: classrooms where teachers are handed, or mandated to design, scripted daily lesson plans that are tightly linked to every literary term and stock writing formula for the genres that are the focus of "the test."

In environments like these, teachers are denied their professional expertise to teach uniquely to the students within their classrooms. The languages, literacy practices, and cultural knowledge that students already possess and that can help them grow academically are held hostage at the classroom door. Teacher candidates despair about whether or how they can possibly bring to life the visions of teaching and learning they are crafting. Transnationalism impresses on us the urgency of returning professional expertise to teachers to design educational approaches in which we and our students draw upon the rich linguistic and cultural knowledge and skill sets of transnational *and* mononational students, who are also diverse, and who sit beside transnational students in classrooms (Hamann et al., 2006; Sánchez, 2007a, 2007b, 2009; Skerrett, 2012a; Zúñiga & Hamann, 2009; Zúñiga, Hamann, & Sánchez García, 2008).

Research that I and others have conducted examines the special and powerful transnational knowledge and understandings, and the multiliterate, multilingual, and transcultural repertoires, that transnational youths develop as a consequence of transnational life (Sánchez, 2007a, 2007b, 2009; Skerrett, 2012a, 2013; Skerrett & Bomer, 2013). Transnational youths' resources often include knowledge and skills in two or more languages and cultures, and two or more social, educational, economic, and political national contexts. My introductory profile of Cameron suggests how he purposefully capitalized on knowledge of two transnational contexts to build his musical knowledge, experiences, and literacies. Vanesa, Cameron, Monica, and other transnational youths I have worked with often speak two or more formal languages (Spanish, Dutch, French, and English) as well as varieties of those languages—for instance, the "Frenglish" that youths in St. Martin explained to me is a French-English mixing akin to Spanglish.

Transnational youths' capacities further include knowing when and how to draw from, combine, and reshape these cultural and linguistic repertoires to cross borders and achieve success in distinct domains of particular national contexts (for example, school or social life). For instance, Vanesa's initial experience of U.S. schooling was characterized by social isolation and academic confusion. She told me how "it was hard for me in the beginning because I didn't know much English." Vanesa linked her ability to extend her friendship groups outside her ESL community of Spanish-dominant peers to her growing English skills, telling me, "I started talking more English and then I have a lot of friends." Furthermore, as Vanesa formed friendships with Mexican American peers, she began talking and texting with them in Spanglish, which signaled and maintained their cultural and linguistic identities. She told me, "I text in Spanish with some of my friends but it's weird because we mix the Spanish and English."

From this brief examination of the resources and skill sets that youths develop from transnational living, we can agree that these capabilities are vital for productively living in, and contributing to, an increasingly cosmopolitan, globalized world. Zúñiga and Hamann (2009) characterized the transnational knowledge sets and capacities that youths stand to accrue from this lifestyle as great benefits, writing,

> For some, being a transnational student is or will become an asset; they gain proficiency in the languages, cultural mores, and means of living in more than one national context and thereby have broader opportunity horizons than their mononational peers. (pp. 332–333)

These transnational knowledge sets and capacities are attractive and beneficial for all students to acquire, whether they live across two or more countries or in one nation alone. Yet these competencies are typically invisible in literacy classrooms and thus are not considered resources for teaching and learning. More than that, transnational youths find few substantive opportunities, in or outside school, to build or maintain the transnational linguistic, cultural, sociopolitical, and other forms of understandings and skills they need to be successful at transnational life (Skerrett, 2012a). Engaging with transnationalism in literacy education can generate knowledge and capacities in transnational as well as mononational students that will equip them to engage productively in social, economic, and political life in ways that are deeply and critically informed by a transnational outlook.

Research also details the significant educational challenges that stem from transnational life, difficulties that are typically poorly understood and largely unaddressed from the purview of literacy classrooms. The thorniest problem is that transnational youths take frequent and/or extended stays in one country and its schools, necessarily making them absent from schools in another country (Hamann et al., 2006; Zúñiga et al., 2008). Unique academic challenges arise for these transnational youths and their teachers as they navigate education across multiple languages, cultures, and sociopolitical contexts. My ongoing research is uncovering many of these specialized hardships. For instance, some transnational youths struggle academically in one schooling context because the language of education is a language they are still learning. There are often different curricular emphases and instructional approaches in the two educational contexts in which they go to school, making their academic learning and performance across contexts uneven. Sometimes there are also quite different cultural norms governing teacher–student interactions across international contexts, introducing social problems and disciplinary issues for these students and their teachers. Teachers need a robust set of educational approaches through which to navigate these challenges. Such approaches would include, for example, preparing with transnational students for leave-takings; supporting, and staying abreast of, formal learning that may be occurring for them in another country; keeping students growing in the knowledge and skills they have been developing in the educational context from which they are departing; and reintegrating transnational students into the learning communities they have left.

There is a strong body of literacy research with sound implications for educational practice that addresses these issues in relation to immigrant youths. Research has lighted pathways for teachers to assist their immigrant students in becoming adept in the languages, cultures, mores, and instructional approaches of their new country, while supporting the youths' academic and sociocultural development in the linguistic, cultural, and literacy practices of their homes and communities (e.g., Fu & Graff, 2009; Martínez, 2010; Martínez-Roldán & Fránquiz, 2009). But transnational youths present a distinctively different challenge because they continue to be formally educated across different countries and thus must become increasingly skilled in the languages, cultures, and curriculums of two or more nations (or even different regions within different countries). Hamann (2001) called these "extra acculturative challenges" (p. 38) for sojourner students who "need not only learn how to negotiate this new place (i.e., the community surrounding their present school), but more fundamentally *any* new place, as the prospect looms that they will sooner or later be headed someplace else" (Zúñiga & Hamann, 2009, p. 330).

Beyond the curricular, linguistic, and cultural differences of transnational schools, dissimilar educational policies and political landscapes across countries further shape the quality and degree of access to formal education for transnational youths. For instance, some youths have access to high-quality public schooling in TC 1 whereas in TC 2 the publicly funded schools are of low quality and students' families cannot afford the costs of private schooling. Some countries require parents to pay for textbooks and other expensive educational materials that another nation might provide free of charge to its youths. Extra costs of this kind can make education less accessible to youths in countries where education is not fully subsidized. Thus, transnational scholars conclude that national school systems "are not deliberately designed to consider the needs, understandings, and wants of an increasingly international, mobile population" (Zúñiga & Hamann, 2009, p. 329).

By posing such generative resources and serious challenges for transnational youths and their literacy education, transnationalism presents us as educators with an urgent need to envision and enact approaches to teaching and learning that are more aware of, and responsive to, the phenomenon of transnational life as experienced by our students. I build such transnational approaches to literacy education in this book. In thinking through literacy education that is responsive to transnational life, I lean on established approaches in which teachers plan for teaching and learning with knowledge of our students in mind—their reading and writing interests, abilities, and learning needs; their home cultures, languages, and outside-school literacy practices and activities; and the personal, social, and political issues that affect them, their families, and their communities (Bomer, 2011; Gonzalez, Moll, & Amanti, 2005; Kinloch, 2009; Martínez, 2010; Skerrett, 2011). Transnationalism, and the associated resources, capacities, and challenges it produces for youths, should inform literacy education in the same way that we've already recognized that students' local cultures, languages, literacy practices, and experiences should.

This book is important and necessary for literacy educators and scholars because, although we have many texts that offer theory and examples of practice to guide teachers in attending to students' cultures, languages, and outside-school literate lives in their curriculum and teaching (e.g., Bomer, 2011; Kinloch, 2009, 2011), we have no such explicit examples in relation to transnationalism. This absence presents a worrisome gap in literacy theory and educational practice as the number of transnational youths is growing rapidly in schools around the world. Zúñiga and Hamann (2009) have cautioned that if we and our teaching overlook the national, cultural, linguistic, and other pluralisms of our transnational students, then "transnational experience [becomes] a drawback because it places [transnational youths] between cultures and behind mononational peers in academic proficiency, a dynamic that can spiral into school failure" (pp. 332–333). If we do not intentionally seek out our transnational students' knowledge, experiences, and capabilities, and position those as resources for literacy education, our educational practices will become part of the " inhibiting factors . . . that limit some transnationals' willingness to *imagine* themselves as fully part of their current environs" (Hamann et al., 2006, p. 264). Our transnational students will more likely see themselves as "students *between* two nations rather than *of* two nations" and have a "plural or partial sense of belonging" (emphasis in original, Hamann et al., p. 264). Just as with all of our diverse students, we want to ensure that our teaching supports, rather than inhibits, our transnational students' sense of belonging in our classrooms.

I offer this book as a beginning vision of how attention to transnationalism can fit within the work we already do with our diverse students and make it even more productive. By foregrounding transnationalism as an informant of literacy education, the book offers research-based approaches that will allow us, along with our students, to learn about the transnational experiences, knowledge, and language and literacy skills our students and communities possess. Through explicit instructional approaches and activities, the book further guides us into using what we learn about our students' transnational lifestyles and capacities as a resource for deepening and expanding the literacy teaching and learning that is already happening in our classrooms.

THE PEOPLE AND GEOGRAPHIES IN RESEARCH INFORMING THE BOOK

This book integrates the voices and experiences of transnational students and their literacy teachers from three research projects investigating student diversity and literacy education in parts of the United States, Canada, and the Caribbean. All three projects employed qualitative research methods of interviews, observations, and collection of documents and artifacts, as well as analytic procedures combining elements of grounded theory and thematic analysis (Charmaz, 2000; Glaser & Strauss, 2006; Miles & Huberman, 1994). Although the projects were designed to focus on particular geographies, the nature of the questions I asked and the student populations around which they were framed led me to notice a range of other national contexts—spanning African and Asian countries, Central and South America, Europe, and Mexico—that were implicated in the literate lives and education of diverse youths. Comparing these three projects led me to notice their primary point of connection: increasing racial, cultural, and linguistic diversity in literacy classrooms, including as manifested by the growing demographic of transnational youths, and the curricular responses of literacy teachers to their diversifying student bodies.

PRIMARY EDUCATIONAL THEORIES INFORMING THE BOOK

One of the key insights my research provides is the notion that experiences of crossing borders and dwelling at borderzones—hybrid places where borders intersect—are significant in learning, development, and change (Skerrett, 2012a; Skerrett & Bomer, 2011, 2013). The concepts of crossing borders and inhabiting borderzones include physical, psychological, ideological, and other dimensions. For instance, a transnational youth who thinks of his national identity as straddling two or more nations can be understood as inhabiting a borderzone that is psychological in nature. In this book, I use theories of border crossing and borderzones (Anzaldúa, 1987; Bakhtin, 1981; Bhabha, 1994; Guerra, 2007; Rosaldo, 1989; Skerrett & Bomer, 2011, 2013) to examine how transnational youths' experiences of crossing borders or inhabiting borderzones generate learning, change, development, and hybridity in their identities, cultures, and language and literacy practices. I both theorize and illustrate how teachers and students can capitalize upon the experiences and repertoires associated with transnational border crossings and borderzones by adopting a form of literacy education that more consciously includes transnational youths. Another key insight of this book is that teachers and students can design curriculum and instructional practices that purposively recruit the resources for literacy education that transnational students bring to our classrooms for the benefit of all of our diverse students. I ground this insight and related approaches through which we can take on this work in the New London Group's (1996) theory of a pedagogy of multiliteracies and Arnetha Ball's (2009) conception of teachers' generativity in culturally and linguistically complex classrooms (CLCCs).

Border Crossings and Borderzones

Transnational youths like those profiled in this book move across national boundaries of the United States and Canada, Caribbean islands, Mexico, and African, Asian, and European countries. These geographical boundaries are often understood to separate languages, cultures, relationships, roles, and literacy practices. Thus, physical, political, linguistic, cultural, social, and ideological boundaries are just some of the borders that are typically inscribed or perceived among the national geographies in which transnational youths lead their lives. Yet those boundaries are not absolute, strictly delineated, or unalterable (Orellana, 2007). Instead, they are blurred, hybrid, and changeable (Anzaldúa, 1987; Bakhtin, 1981; Bhabha, 1994; Guerra, 2007; Gutiérrez, 2008; Rosaldo, 1989) for and by the people who interact with them. Moreover, rather than simply serving as opportunities to cross over (or be turned away), borders create hybrid spaces called borderzones, or places where different contexts intersect. These borderzones are potentially generative sites for new and powerful forms of learning, development, and change (Anzaldúa, 1987; Guerra, 2007; Gutiérrez, 2008; Rosaldo, 1989; Skerrett & Bomer, 2011, 2013).

Randy Bomer and I (Skerrett & Bomer, 2013) have written about how the transnational students in a literacy classroom in Austin, Texas, under the encouragement and guidance of their literacy teacher, Molly Campbell, drew on their transcultural identities and hybrid language and literacy practices to create multilingual and multimodal texts that bore the themes of border crossing and borderzone existences. Kris Gutiérrez (2008), who studied an educational program for the children of migrant workers, also recognized that the youths traversed daily multiple contexts—their local neighborhoods, their transnational communities, and the educational program that was housed at a prestigious university—each of which bore its own distinct spatial, ideological, and cultural dimensions. Gutiérrez (2008) theorized the educational program as a transformative "Third Space" because it merged and addressed the academic and social concerns of students and their communities and facilitated their development of a range of language and literacy skills. This book positions teachers and students as agents who identify, analyze, challenge, and learn from the borders, including those that characterize transnational life, that we or others have created among the different spaces of our literate lives. It invites us to reconstitute borders as blurred and changeable spaces in which we can locate our teaching and our students' learning.

Importantly, all of our students—not just those from transnational or certain immigrant, ethnic, and linguistic backgrounds—pass through a variety of borderzones in daily life. Rosaldo (1989) defined borderlands as those spaces not just along national boundaries but also "at less formal intersections, such as those of gender, age, status, and distinctive life experiences" (p. 29). He "consider[ed] the disparate worlds one passes through in daily life, a round that includes home, eating out, working hours, adventures in consumerland, and a range of relationships, from intimacy to collegiality and friendship to enmity," concluding that "encounters with cultural and related differences belong to all of us in our most mundane experiences . . ." (Rosaldo, 1989, pp. 29–30). These arguments suggest that all our students, not just those who live across national geographies, are border crossers and develop hybrid social, cultural, linguistic, and literate identities and practices as a result. This proposition further means that all our students will benefit from literacy pedagogy that recruits their experiences, knowledge, and skills of navigating and dwelling at various kinds of borders and borderzones as tools for engaging in academic work. In a reciprocal manner, such forms of teaching and learning should facilitate our students' development of an array of linguistic, literacy, sociocultural, and other kinds of knowledge and capacities they need to navigate a variety of borders and borderlands across multiple areas of life. I work from two theories of literacy pedagogy, the New London Group's (1996) theory of a pedagogy of multiliteracies and Arnetha Ball's (2009) theory of teachers' generativity in culturally and linguistically complex classrooms, that illuminate how we can identify and engage the diverse and hybrid identities, experiences, knowledge, and language and literacy practices that our students accrue from living within, at, and across borders for literacy education.

A Pedagogy of Multiliteracies

Transnational and other youths' transactions with many social, cultural, language, and literacy practices across varied borders align with a sociocultural view of literacy as a constellation of multimodal practices situated within multiple social contexts and activities (Barton, Hamilton, & Ivanic, 2000; New London Group, 1996). From this perspective, what it means to be literate depends upon the contexts, purposes, tools, and skill sets available for making meaning. People engage in literate activity for wide-ranging purposes: to achieve private, civic, social, academic, economic, and cultural goals. Furthermore, in a view of literacy as social practice, language and literacy practices are interconnected. The New London Group challenged the concept of "mere literacy" (1996, p. 64), arguing that its primary failure was that it centered only on language, and often, on a stable form of one language. In place of mere literacy, these scholars proposed "multiliteracies" (New London Group, 1996, p. 64), an idea that acknowledged other modes of representation that were culture- and context-specific and broader than language alone. Multiliteracies are representational resources that people use to achieve multiple goals across myriad social contexts including linguistic, visual, audio, gestural, spatial, and multimodal patterns of meaning—this last combining two or more of the preceding elements. Reminding us of the many social contexts and borders that populate literate life, the New London Group (1996) further proposed that representational resources include lifeworlds—structured spaces, contexts, or discourse communities that possess cultural, historical, ideological, spatial, and other dimensions.

The New London Group's (1996) theorization of multiliteracies came in response to mounting cultural and linguistic diversity in societies, an increasingly globalized world, rapidly advancing technologies, and proliferating subcultural diversity in which individuals create subcommunities according to shared interests and worldviews. This imperative signals the many ways in which our students are diverse and allows us to view our transnational students, as well as their mononational peers, as multicultural, multilingual (speaking one or more official languages and their different social forms), and multiliterate. Speaking to literacy educators, the New London Group (1996) theorized a pedagogy of multiliteracies that could enable learners to productively access their and others' diversity so as to contribute to, and benefit from, their local and global communities.

A pedagogy of multiliteracies (New London Group, 1996) directs us to create opportunities for our students and ourselves to learn about the many different languages and literacies within our classrooms, and the contexts of practice to which they are connected. This pedagogical approach invites us to guide our students into exploring the different ways in which they use their language and literacy practices to make meaning of life and to be people in the world, as well as to consider social, cultural, political, and other influences on how they choose to practice their languages and literacies. Moreover, a pedagogy of multiliteracies encourages us and our students to transform the nature of literacy education in school by infusing it with the many goals our students hold for language and literacy learning, including for their endeavors with language and literacy in outside-school contexts. There is some research containing exemplary models of literacy teachers drawing upon and building up their diverse students' language and literacy practices for academic and other forms of literacy learning and engagement both in and outside school (see, for example, Fisher, 2005; Morrell, 2002; Skerrett, 2012b; Skerrett & Bomer, 2011). Randy and I, for example, drawing from our study in Molly Campbell's classroom, have shown how Campbell and her students drew upon students' outside-school meaning-making practices, such as digital communications with their cellphones and analytic processes with television shows and movies, to read, understand, analyze, and critique academic texts (Skerrett & Bomer, 2011). In this book, I will also draw upon the framework of multiliteracies pedagogy in designing ways we can learn about and employ our transnational and other diverse students' language and literacy repertoires for literacy learning in school, learning that will also support their literate lives in outside-school settings.

Teachers' Generativity in Culturally and Linguistically Complex Classrooms

As with a pedagogy of multiliteracies (New London Group, 1996), Arnetha Ball's (2009) theory of generativity positions us and our students as agents who can teach and learn with awareness of the contexts in and across which our students live and the resources for literacy education that are inherent within students and those communities. Ball (2009) coined the term *culturally and linguistically complex classrooms* (CLCCs) to describe classrooms that serve students from two or more cultural and linguistic groups. In keeping with the topic of this book, I would also add students who hold multiple national affiliations. Because the demographic makeup of these classrooms is constantly changing, and teachers can never fully know or share the cultural and linguistic backgrounds of their students, Ball asserted that we must develop generativity for teaching in CLCCs. Generativity means that as teachers, we add to our understanding of how to meet students' educational needs by connecting our personal and professional knowledge with our students' knowledge in ways that produce new knowledge that is useful in curricular planning and pedagogical problem solving.

I drew on Ball's (2009) conception of generative teachers in the instructional approaches developed in this book for teaching with awareness of the transnational youths who comprise a demographic of diversity in our CLCCs. I first took up Ball's (2009) theory in my research into how teachers thought about and responded, through their curricular and instructional practices, to their students' diversity. Heather, the Canadian teacher whose voice and classroom you will hear and look into in Chapter 2, enacted generativity in learning about the myriad forms of national, cultural, and linguistic diversity her students represented; creating a transnationally affirming learning environment; and assisting students in drawing upon their diversity to meet academic objectives.

Conceptualizing teaching in response to transnationalism through Ball's (2009) terms, teachers become *metacognitively aware* of our students' lived experiences and language and literacy practices, including those of our transnational students that occur across nations. We experience *ideological becoming* by developing our stances on how teaching and learning in our classrooms will be affected by our students' lives, including those that are transnational existences. Through the process of *internalization*, we acquire knowledge and critical perspectives on transnationalism and other circumstances of our diverse students' lives, noting the resources for literacy education that they procure and the challenges that emerge that we can address proactively. In the continuous process of *generativity*, we will always be learning about our students' transnational and local communities and engagements with language and literacy, in order to combine that knowledge with our professional expertise and theoretical knowledge to design curricular and instructional responses to the unique dilemmas that will arise in our ever-evolving CLCCs.

ORGANIZATION OF THE BOOK AND OVERVIEW OF THE CHAPTERS

The book is organized into six chapters that progressively build an approach to foregrounding transnationalism in literacy education for the benefit of both transnational students and their mononational classmates. Each of the chapters to come opens with the voices and experiences of a transnational youth or teacher of transnational students or a classroom interaction that highlights the particular concepts being explored in that chapter. I then relate these student experiences and classroom interactions to educational research and theories that are relevant to the foci of each chapter, and to insights from my own research. The final portion of each chapter offers curricular and instructional suggestions that we can take up in our classrooms to address the dimensions of transnationally aware literacy education treated in the chapter. In making these suggestions, I integrate shorter portraits, vignettes, descriptions, and examples from my research showing how we, our students, and other educational stakeholders can undertake the proposed work in literacy education. Through this approach, I hope to help us understand the theoretical and research bases for the approach of the book, connect the book's approach to our lived experiences with transnational and other students in our classrooms, and envision how attending to transnationalism can practically and productively inform teaching and learning in our classrooms and also help us support youths' literacy development in other spaces of literate life.

Chapter 2 explores the forms of knowledge, experiences, and language and literacy practices that youths develop in transnational life. It conceptualizes these transnational resources within the total set of educational resources diverse students bring to school and details how these transnational repertoires may contribute to literacy teaching and learning. The chapter also illuminates the presence of transnational youths in our schools and classrooms and suggests approaches through which we can inquire into all of our students' lived experiences and repertoires for learning—approaches that will also lead us to discover the transnational knowledge, languages, and literacies that our students possess. Chapter 2 positions teachers and students as researchers of our own lives and our local and global communities who can investigate, identify, and document our transnational knowledge and experiences and language and literacy practices.

Chapter 3 integrates transnationalism into classroom life by examining how our students' transnational knowledge, experiences, languages, and literacy practices (along with the diverse repertoires of all our students) can assist the teaching and learning processes and meet the academic objectives of literacy classrooms. I discuss theories of curriculum as ideological, political, official, and enacted and take us through sound approaches to teaching and learning in literacy classrooms—reading, writing, and critical inquiry—into which we can invest our students' forms of experience, knowledge and languages and literacies, including those of our transnational students. The chapter also offers a set of generative questions through which we and our students can remain mindfully aware, across a school year, of how students' transnational repertoires can assist in teaching and learning the official curriculum and facilitate our achievement of other goals as literate people.

Chapter 4 faces head-on the challenge posed by the fact that some transnational students' formal schooling occurs across two or more countries. I explore key knowledge and understandings that teachers of transnational youths need to acquire about the transnational educational settings that are most immediately relevant for them and their students, and I also suggest some approaches and activities for learning about those settings. Chapter 4 further discusses how teachers, students, and families can plan together for transitioning in and out of transnational school settings, thus reducing some of the educational ruptures that transnational youths currently experience. I outline some approaches and activities in which we can respectively engage to support our students and their families as they plan for and execute those transitions. Finally, I discuss the importance of teaching with an awareness of the educational lives of transnational youths as those lives unfold in other contexts, and suggest some ways we can stay abreast of, and involved in, our transnational students' learning in other countries. Although this chapter foregrounds transnational educational movements and ruptures, I recognize that transnational as well as mononational students sometimes experience intranational movements across schools. Thus, the ideas in Chapter 4 apply to all teachers who seek to stay informed of and involved in their students' education within their classrooms as well as in other educational settings.

Chapter 5 addresses another challenge of transnational education—the interruption of formal schooling that sometimes occurs when transnational youths cross borders. This chapter examines how we can sponsor and support the literacy development of transnational youths in nonschool settings. I identify a variety of formal and informal spaces across transnational settings in which youths participate in literate life and highlight the significant literacy learning that they achieve in those spaces. As in the other chapters, I conceptualize the work of supporting our transnational students' outside-school literate lives within a broader approach in which we learn about and sponsor all of our students' literacy development in the contexts outside school that are significant for them. I detail some approaches and activities that we can employ to learn from our students about the diverse spaces of their transnational and mononational literate lives. The chapter also outlines how we can support and guide our transnational students, as we do with all our students, in purposefully building their language and literacy practices in nonschool settings.

A brief concluding chapter frames teaching with awareness of transnationalism as a socially just and equity-minded response given the growing numbers of transnational students in schools around the world. It also reminds us of the unique and important outcomes and gains that all our students, regardless of their transnational status, will achieve from engaging with transnationalism in literacy education.

CHAPTER 2

Becoming Transnationally Literate

Now that we're familiar with the idea of transnationalism, we have a working understanding of the growing presence and impact of transnationalism in societies, families, and schools around the world, and how transnationalism shapes the social and educational experiences of youths. Beginning with this chapter, I use the phrase *becoming transnationally literate* to capture our process, already under way, of acquiring knowledge and understandings about transnationalism and transnational youths in social life and in education. The goal of this chapter is to help us become more transnationally literate. To do so, we will dig deeper into the experiences, knowledge, and perspectives, and language and literacy repertoires that youths develop through transnational lifestyles. These repertoires provide a powerful potential resource for literacy education. We will envision how they might contribute to the already visible resources for teaching and learning that all our students bring to school.

TRANSNATIONAL RESOURCES AVAILABLE FOR LITERACY EDUCATION

Transnational youths develop a wealth of knowledge and language and literacy capacities that are useful for literacy education. We can intentionally set out to discover our transnational students' repertoires for learning and integrate them, conceptually and practically, into the broader set of learning resources that whole groups of our diverse students bring to school.

Transnational Knowledge and Capabilities

Transnational youths and their families develop specialized knowledge, worldviews, and capabilities from living across two or more nations. For example, transnational families and their children develop and strategically use knowledge about how a transnational lifestyle can build and maximize cross-national political, cultural, educational, and linguistic capital. Vanesa's family, as we have seen, deliberately arranged a transnational lifestyle that allowed the father to continue working in Mexico at a lucrative family business while enabling the children to access educational benefits from living in the United States. The children and mother's frequent and extended return trips to Mexico helped them maintain deep family and cultural ties to their homeland while they were also adding new cultural and linguistic repertoires by living in the United States. Other transnational families build economic strength by strategically choosing places and times for migration to capitalize on employment opportunities in one land and stretching out those earnings by living in a country with a lower cost of living for specified periods (Zúñiga & Hamann, 2009).

Transnational families and youths also acquire and execute transnational knowledge in terms of securing love and care for children. They come to think flexibly about transnational living arrangements for children with different configurations of family that are stretched across nations and involve extended kin (Bledsoe & Sow, 2011; Coe et al., 2011). Cameron's family thought in such pliable ways about family, allowing Cameron to move to New York and live with an aunt there as he completed secondary education in a high school that focused on the musical literacies he was gifted at and passionate about. Such forms of knowledge, perspectives, and capacities allow families and youths to maximize life by living it transnationally.

Transnational youths also acquire and deploy intercultural knowledge, understandings, skills, dispositions, and flexibility in transnational living (Canagarajah, 2006, 2009; Hamann et al., 2006; Sánchez, 2007a, 2007b, 2009; Skerrett, 2012a; Zúñiga & Hamann, 2009). Sánchez (2009) defined cultural flexibility as the ability of transnational youths to respond dynamically to the social and cultural ways of being in different cultural contexts. Vanesa, for instance, developed cultural flexibility that allowed her to identify, analyze, and value different cultural beliefs and practices across her Mexican and U.S. worlds and develop her own perspectives on youths' positions and agency in families, schools, and societies. As she explained:

> I discovered too much here [in the United States] . . . like I didn't know I would draw or dance. It's just like in Mexico, like what your parents teach you and what is at home is just like, whatever they like tell you, you have to do it. . . . For example, I was in swimming classes and my grandma always went for me and picked me up and stuff like that. But it was because she wanted to. And I like[d] it. I enjoy[ed] it. I don't blame her for that. But it's like sometimes you have to discover things and I think here [the United States] is like the best place . . . [for] stuff like that.

Global citizenship is another significant worldview and identity that transnational youths often develop. Sánchez (2007a) defined global citizenship as the ability to hold empathies and insights that cut across local and national borders, maintain a sense of civic responsibility to the international community, and understand intersections among local and global economies. Elsewhere, Sánchez (2009) discussed how leading a transnational life affords youths an in-depth kind of world learning, a transnational literacy that she and other scholars (e.g., Canagarajah, 2006, 2009) have asserted cannot be acquired by participation in just one sociopolitical or sociocultural context. Cameron developed a strong mindset as a critical global citizen from his extensive transnational sojourns during his childhood and teenage years. Beyond St. Martin, St. Maarten, and New York, Cameron's family's transnational ties also expanded to Europe. He had spent time with family members who lived in France and had traveled to Italy as well. Cameron and his family had also visited a number of Caribbean islands, including Dominica, Belize, Honduras, St. Kitts, and Barbados.

These international movements gave Cameron a sense of being a citizen of the world with related transnational socioeconomic and sociopolitical perspectives and critiques. For example, Cameron compared Dominica to St. Maarten and other European and U.S. cities as "really natural, not as urbanized." Grasping the diversity that comprised the Caribbean rather than the monolithic character that people often ascribe to this part of the world, Cameron noted, "I really admired and I was really grateful to be there [Dominica] to see how different the Caribbean could be." He critiqued his family's comfortable economic position relative to poorer Central American families', a privilege that allowed him to "come off of a fancy cruise and visit places that a lot of homeless people" called home, places that transported you "back to . . . the past, a place away from what you are used to."

Such transnational knowledge and perspectives are more easily accessible to transnational youths than to mononational young people, given transnational youths' broader world experiences. Yet these forms of knowledge and understandings are beneficial for all youths, not just transnational students. For instance, the cultural flexibility, sense of global citizenship, and the abilities to build, maintain, and use social, economic, and other kinds of cross-national networks are essential for all people in an increasingly globalized world, and, as Gee (2006) noted, in a fast-changing capitalist society. Couching his discussion in terms of equity, Gee (2006) urged educators to foster these characteristics and skills in all students, not just those from dominant social groups.

Transnational Linguistic Resources

Language is a distinct form of knowledge attended by its own practices, even though linguistic repertoires (which include knowledge, understandings, and beliefs about language, as well as the actual practices/usages of language) are embedded within people's broader social and cultural knowledge and practices (Gee, 1999). This means we should pay specific and careful attention to the linguistic knowledge, beliefs, and practices that transnational as well as mononational youths develop as they live across different national and cultural geographies (Ball, 2009; Canagarajah, 2006, 2009; García & Gaddes, 2012; Martínez, 2010; Sánchez, 2007a, 2007b; Skerrett, 2012a). Canagarajah (2006, 2009) identified many aspects of transnational youths' linguistic repertoires. These include the skills of interpersonal communication, the ability to monitor the forms and conventions that multiple speakers bring to communication, and performance strategies that enable a speaker's oral language to be more fully understood by a particular cultural/

linguistic audience. Transnational linguistic repertoires also include purposeful uses of language developed by multilingual speakers in transnational contact situations. One such purposeful use of language is code meshing, where "students bring in their preferred varieties in rhetorically strategic ways resulting in a hybrid text containing divergent varieties of English" (Canagarajah, 2006, p. 598). Canagarajah's (2006, 2009) and others' work (Martínez, 2010; Orellana & Reynolds, 2008; Skerrett, 2012a; Sutherland, 2008; V. Young, 2007) also draws attention to the concept of language ideologies: the social, cultural, and political beliefs about and attitudes toward various languages that shape students' (and schools') language practices.

Using Vanesa as an example in Chapter 1, I displayed the impressive scope of a bilingual transnational youth's linguistic repertoires and how she wielded these tools to develop relationships across social groups that differed in the extent of their national, cultural, and linguistic affiliations with English and Spanish. Vanesa's language practices within and across social groups were shaped by her developing beliefs and views about the significance and value of different languages in particular social contexts. As we saw earlier, Vanesa thought it was "weird" that she and her Mexican and Mexican American friends used more English than Spanish in their code-switching practices. When I probed Vanesa about the reasons underlying her choices and uses of different languages, she expressed uncertainty about the causes, implying that she was not fully aware about the language ideologies that drove her toward greater usage of English and away from her native language.

Beyond social relations, Vanesa also capitalized on her expanding linguistic repertoires for academic success in the United States. She chose French as an elective in high school because, having learned English, she was confident in her ability to learn another language. She offered me this reasoning about which language to take as an elective course: "Well, first I was like, 'I want to take Spanish because it's easy and I know Spanish.' But then I was like, 'Why should I take Spanish if I know Spanish? Let's go for another language.'" Vanesa explained to me that learning French was "hard, though. But I mean learning another language or something else is like the same process." She noted, for instance, that "There [are] some words that you can really link with Spanish and stuff."

Moreover, Vanesa continued to use Spanish extensively at home to maintain family closeness and their linguistic and cultural identity, even as her mother encouraged the family to speak more English at home. The desire for more English at home seemed driven by Vanesa's mother's language ideology that linguistic capital in English was crucial to the children's academic and social success in the United States. Vanesa told me how,

> My mom is always telling me that we should speak English all the time [at home]. So my little brother can hear us and learn more words and stuff like that. But we usually speak Spanish. Or sometimes we mix the language [but] there's more Spanish than English.

All people, not just those who speak two or more official languages, strategically vary their uses of language(s) depending on the social contexts, participants, beliefs about language, and goals in a given communication situation (Gee, 1999; V. Young, 2007). Vanesa pointed out the diverse forms of the English language she encountered in the United States as she traveled from a predominantly White middle school to Southwest High School, which served a culturally and linguistically diverse student population that included African American, Mexican, and Mexican American youths.

> [My middle school] was a school [with] like very White people and here at Southwest High it's like different people and stuff and they speak like another language. Well, not another language but a slang language [by which she meant African American English] and I didn't know those words. And like, well, people in my other school, like White kids and stuff, they didn't speak like that.

We can think of the linguistic repertoires our transnational students possess as part of the total set of linguistic resources our students bring to school that can be useful for teaching and learning. Much research shows the richness and complexity of languages such as African American English and the new shared language practices diverse youths create from engaging together in communities of language and literacy practice like schools (Paris, 2011; V. Young, 2007). Deepening our understandings of the sophisticated nature of all our students' language practices, including those of transnational students, will further orient us toward viewing students' linguistic repertoires as strengths and as teaching and learning tools that we can enlist in their education. Furthermore, as part of our literacy curriculum, we can study the complex and critical nature of language usage in our students' lives, including their beliefs about language, or language ideologies, that derive from and drive their language practices. Such inquiries, which we will explore later in this chapter, will help our students become more aware of the ways they are using their languages, including how their beliefs about their own and other people's languages shape their language practices. Such a language education will further enable students to become more critical and purposeful in their language practices.

Transnational Multiliteracies Practices

Language and literacy practices are inextricably interconnected. A sociocultural perspective of literacy views literacy as a constellation of multimodal and multilingual tools and practices situated within and across multiple social contexts and activities (Barton et al., 2000; New London Group, 1996). Literacy tools include linguistic, oral, aural, gestural, spatial, and multimodal tools, which combine two or more modes (New London Group, 1996). We can easily point to the physical and online spaces in and outside of school in which our students employ a range of literacy tools such as written language; images; videos that combine oral, aural, gestural, and other literate forms; dance; and art and other forms of expression and communication as indications of their multilingual and multiliteracies practices. Thinking specifically of transnational youths who practice language and literacy across many social contexts in two or more countries allows us to grasp more fully the multiplicity and diversity of spaces that are available for our students to learn and practice their languages and literacies. If we begin by considering only traditional reading and writing acts of literacy, we can readily recognize (and I briefly showed this in the case of my own family) that transnationalism introduces special reading and writing practices for youths and adults (de la Piedra, 2010; Jiménez et al., 2009; Rubinstein-Ávila, 2007; Viera, 2011). Travel, financial, relational, religious, and other activities encompassing two or more nations and cultures necessitate unique reading, writing, and other literacy practices that often involve two or more languages and knowledge of and navigation across multiple cultures.

Reading and writing across two or more national contexts, languages, and cultures can lead to transnational perspectives on how literacy practices are shaped by geography, culture, space, movement, and time. Vanesa, for example, described how she had grown in her identity and practices as a reader by living in the United States. She credited this change to being introduced to "good books" in her reading class and to her teacher continuously encouraging students to read. Vanesa reasoned that the limited availability of books in her small hometown in Mexico had likely curtailed her and her community's engagement with reading. "Here [in the United States], I think they have more access to libraries and they have, like, more books. And over there in Mexico they do have like libraries but I don't know. They just like . . . don't pull you to read."

Vanesa's mother, Luce, also described changes that occurred in her reading practices at home with her younger daughter when they took up transnational living. Luce attributed those changes to cultural differences between her region of Mexico and the United States (rather than the socioeconomic reasoning that Vanesa had offered). Luce contrasted Vanesa's early home literacy practices in Mexico with those of her 5-year-old daughter, Isa, whose early literacy acquisition was occurring in the United States. A significant difference, according to Luce, was that Isa was already reading books on her own: "now that we are here in the States . . . she's reading now. And she's only 5." Luce was regularly reading to Isa as well, and she perceived her younger daughter's early print literacy as a benefit of what she called the "culture" of reading in the United States.

> We don't have that culture [in Mexico]. It's very different. We never read books to the kids. Never. I don't know why. . . . In Mexico, we don't do what they do here. Like [here in the United States] in the night you get a book and you read to the kids.

Displaying the cultural flexibility that empowered her to take on different ways of being in different contexts, Luce commented, "And now I'm getting this culture because I see that it's good for the kids to read since [they're] little and then they keep reading, reading, reading, growing up, and they get a lot of stuff."

Vanesa also took up writing practices as a direct consequence of her transnational lifestyle. She kept a diary, a gift from her mother, who understood that taking on a transnational lifestyle would be transformative for her daughter, and worth remembering. Vanesa explained:

> I just started my diary when I came [to the U.S.]. My mom gave me a diary, a notebook . . . and then she was like, "What happen[s] to you here is going to be a new experience for you. And you can write it down so you can remember whatever happened to you here."

Suggesting the salience of chronicling and reflecting on her transnational experience, Vanesa faithfully wrote in her diary. "I started writing in it when I came. And I still write everything that happens still now. Like every weekend . . . if like something happened in the school like important, I just wr[ite] it down." Language variation was a prominent feature of Vanesa's literacy work of journal writing. Vanesa's diary was itself a material artifact of shifting language practices. "Like in my diary, I just started like writing in it and it was in Spanish and then it's like mixed with the Spanish and English and then it's all English." When I asked if she ever reverted to Spanish or Spanish-English mixing, Vanesa replied, "Not really. I just write in English." Probing again into her language ideologies as manifested in her writing, I asked Vanesa why she thought she was now only writing in English in her diary. She replied, "I think because I got the language, I guess. I don't know. That's weird." I wondered aloud to her whether she might have become more comfortable writing in English than Spanish but she was not sure that this was indeed the case, indicated by her wavering response of "Yeah, I think so. I guess. Yeah."

Combining reading, writing, and spoken language with other multiliteracies practices lends an even more sophisticated understanding of what transnational literacies entail. For example, transnational youths increasingly take up digital literacies (new technologies of communication and meaning-making such as cellphones and laptops that youths often, but not always, use to connect to the Internet and "online" spaces). For transnational youths, "online" access is key to promoting their participation in globally inclusive lives, learning new languages, and accessing transcultural and other social identities (e.g., Black, 2005, 2009; Canagarajah, 2006, 2009; Lam, 2004, 2006; Lam & Rosario-Ramos, 2009; Lam & Warriner, 2012; Yi, 2008). Online communities often serve as a way for transnational youths to remain connected to, and even strengthen, membership in their communities of origin while socializing into new ones and developing old and new language and literacy practices. Vanesa and other transnational youths that I have worked with rely on Facebook, Instant Messaging, virtual communities where the language of communication is one other than English, and other digital spaces and communication tools to maintain transnational friendships and their cultural and linguistic identities and practices.

Vanesa, for example, explained how she

> visits a Spanish website and they have quizzes and stuff and tests, like loving tests and friendship tests. . . . Every day when I'm on Facebook . . . I just open that website and start seeing what's new and stuff like that. On my Facebook I have a lot of messages from a lot of people from Mexico.

Many of our students, whether they hold transnational or mononational identities, use digital literacies, such as Facebook, and other multiliteracies practices to maintain and extend social networks, try on different kinds of identities, and build their skills in particular activities that interest them, whether those include video-gaming (Gee, 2007) or writing fan fiction (Black, 2005; Lam, 2004, 2006; Yi, 2008).

Digital literacies are just one means through which transnational youths develop and display transcultural identities. The newcomer Mexican students to a U.S. high school in Bruna's (2007) study used multiliteracies that involved tagging, branding (drawing attention to clothing or other items on their bodies), and shout-outs (spontaneous shouts of the names of their home states or regions) as informal literacies of display of their communities of origin and emergent transnational identities. These findings reveal a connection to how other diverse mononational youths use tagging to signal their affiliations with particular neighborhoods, "crews," or cultural and linguistic groups (Avramidis & Drakopoulou, 2012; MacGillivray & Curwen, 2007).

My research has shown how other multiliteracies practices such as art, music, and dance can deeply shape people's experiences of transnational life, generate transnational understandings and perspectives, and forge identities and relationships that cut across national, cultural, linguistic, gender, and other boundaries. Vanesa became an avid artist as she lived in the United States, and she, her mother, and her younger sister formed their own affinity group (Gee, 2006) around this practice that strengthened their multiliteracies skills as well as their familial relationship. Vanesa told me:

> I just started liking [drawing] and then I went to Hobby Lobby [an arts and crafts store]. I discovered there are so much things to do if you are creative. . . . I love that. I can stay there for so long. My mom enjoys going to Hobby Lobby too. . . . Yesterday I went to Hobby Lobby and we took so long because my mom liked it too because they have these flowers and she likes a lot of stuff for decorating the house and everything like that. I sometimes ask my mom about what she thinks looks good or what doesn't and stuff like that . . . she's really creative too. My sister, she's really creative. She has a notebook and it's really fat and she has a lot of drawings. She likes to draw a lot and I think she looks at me because I think I'm creative . . . so my mom said that I'm an example for her. So whatever I do, she wants to do it.

Vanesa further described how she showed love for her mother and strengthened their relationship through engaging her multiliteracies art practices.

> Okay, for the Mother's Day: My mom had all these recycle bins like it was full of paper, of JC Penney. You know those magazines? I was like, "Mom, I want to keep that." And she was like, "It's just paper, honey. We don't need it." I was like, "Mom, I just want to keep it." I had an idea to make her a poster. I made this poster for her. And I started cutting all of this stuff like clothes, jewelry, earrings, from the magazines and I put them all in a huge paper and I put "Happy Mother's Day. Everything for the Best Mom." And it's all things that she likes.

Beyond art, Vanesa took up dance at Southwest High, which led her to understand and appreciate African American English and hip-hop music and integrate them into her own identity as a user of languages and literacies.

> Well, when I came here [to Southwest High] I didn't like the music. . . . But then I started liking it. . . . Here the kids, they have a lot of rap music, and then I started listening to it and . . . I started liking it. I don't know why . . . some words that I just like. And also, like the rappers and stuff, they usually write about their life so I think that's kind of cool, like [to] put what you had happen in your life or something like issues they have, they put it in their song. And that's really cool.

Indeed, Vanesa had appropriated hip-hop as her favorite dance form. In one observation of a school dance event, Vanesa was the focal dancer (backed up by two Mexican American girls) in the only hip-hop dance routine of the night.

Thus music literacies are a special avenue through which transnational youths form new affiliations with their culturally and linguistically diverse peers. Earlier, I briefly introduced you to Cameron, who was born in St. Maarten and a passionate musician. Sasha, like Cameron, was another avid musician from St. Maarten with transnational ties to New York. After completing high school in St. Maarten, Sasha chose to attend college in upstate New York. During her first year of college in the United States, Sasha helped create a tightly knit group of international friends who converged around the diversity that made them different from their mostly White, American-born schoolmates. Sasha shared with me how, when she feels homesick for Dutch St. Maarten and French St. Martin, her American Haitian roommate comforts her with Compa and Zook (also spelled Zouk) music that are part of the African Caribbean musical tradition most associated with Haiti.

> I actually have my roommate, even though she is born and raised in the United States, her parents are Haitian. So, sometimes I come to my room, and you know, be like missing home, and I come into my room and she is playing like Zook and Compa, and I am like "YES!" That makes me feel good, the music.

This example beautifully reveals how transnational youths, like other diverse youths (Paris, 2011), stitch together their cultures, multiliteracies, and languages to create new, shared, and in this case, *transnational* cultures, knowledges, and language and literacy practices while affirming their own particular linguistic and cultural identities.

When we, with our students, explore all of our multiliteracies practices together, we create opportunities to define both our individual and collective identities. We can set out to discover our students' multiliteracies practices, knowing that our transnational students will also claim those literacies and that they will likely use them in distinctive ways that support and signal their transnational lifestyles and identities. Learning about all our students' multiliteracies practices is important. Doing so allows us to innovate ways to connect what students already know and do with literacy to the academic literacies and identities we are helping them develop in school (Fisher, 2005; Morrell, 2002; Skerrett & Bomer, 2011, 2013). Let's move now into exploring some instructional approaches that we can enlist to create opportunities for our students to teach us about their multiliterate and multilingual repertoires, and the specialized knowledge and capacities they have built from their life experiences, including transnational lifestyles.

INSTRUCTIONAL APPROACHES FOR BECOMING TRANSNATIONALLY LITERATE

We can use methods such as self-portraiture and related assignments, and inquiry into language and literacy practices across different social contexts, to become literate about our students. All of these exploratory learning activities can be further enhanced by engaging students in critical questioning about their lived experiences and language and literacy practices. One of the key goals of creating such an open and inclusive classroom is to determine which of our students are transnational and to learn more about their educational and broader life experiences. The beginning of the school year is an ideal time for such explorations. It is a time full of expectation, promise, and wonderings. We are eager to learn all about our students and their lives, and we want them to know we are curious about who they are as people in the world, and as learners. Our students also hope we are just that kind of teacher, and that we will make a place for their experiences, knowledge, interests, and questions in this new learning community. As we conduct these explorations into who our students are, the students themselves will lead us to noticings, meaning things that catch their attention or notice (Bomer, 2011), about transnationalism in their lives, in our classrooms, and in our broader communities. We will then adopt a stance of constant awareness of and appreciation for our students' transnational existences—for instance, making our classroom a space where transnationalism lives in our everyday conversations and in the artifacts of the classroom community.

Self-Portraiture

This assignment will work best right at the beginning of the school year and will take up three to four class sessions. We can introduce the self-portraiture activity by telling students it is an opportunity to create a picture of themselves that they want to share with this new learning community—their teacher and their classmates. We would want to inform students as well that beyond building classroom community, the assignment will provide us, their teachers, with important information about the knowledge and skills they have that will be useful for teaching and learning the academic curriculum of our class this year. Handing out the set of guidelines below, or a modified version of it, will guide our students into thinking about their social, cultural, and national identities and their language and literacy knowledge and practices that will be useful for teaching and learning.

In introducing this assignment, the teacher and the class can read through the guidelines and discuss the suggested kinds of information that students might choose to share. The teacher might then allow students to talk further in small groups about their developing ideas for the assignment. Students can then begin working on this assignment for homework that night and come to the next class with a draft that covers at least half of the assignment guidelines. It would work well, also, to provide some or even all of the time in the next class for students to continue working on the assignment. This class time will provide a valuable opportunity for students to talk with their peers about the shared work they are completing—in this way, we will be actively building community and will already be beginning to learn about one another as students conduct this work during class. If this classwork time is provided, students should be able to complete their self-portraits in another evening of homework—although, of course, each teacher will adapt the time needed for completing the assignment depending on the progress students are making.

It will take another one to two class sessions for student presentations of their self-portraits depending on the size of the class and the presentation format. Each student can have about 5 to 7 minutes to present—the idea is to share *from* the self-portrait, not necessarily the entirety of the project, especially if some students' projects become rather expansive. We can think creatively about maximizing time by having students present in roundtable sessions of five to six students. In that way, in a class of 25 students, there will be five presentations occurring simultaneously. (If the noise level is a worry, try securing the library, auditorium, or a grassy spot outdoors ahead of time to hold the presentations.) Another idea to maximize time and students' engagement with their peers' work is to set up the classroom or presentation room as an art gallery. The teacher can stage two or three rounds of a gallery walk where one-third or half of the class can present at individual stations spaced a few feet apart, with the remainder of the class as the audience, who walk around and stop at different viewing stations. The audience can ask questions as they stop by different presenters or leave comment cards with thoughts, noticings, and questions for the presenter. In this way, all students get to share their portraits with at least some of their peers. Furthermore, because the self-portraits are visual and material work, we will be able to keep them on display in the classroom for some time so that students have additional opportunities to engage with their classmates' work.

Students should be assessed in terms of the level of completeness and engagement with the assignment. This assignment is serious academic work. It involves thinking about a variety of potential data to share and making sophisticated decisions about which kinds of data to share, how to combine them, and in what modes to present them. In assessing their work, we will be looking for evidence that students have provided enough information about some aspects of the dimensions we included in the assignment (e.g., literacy activities, language practices, cultural or national background), bearing in mind that we cannot force students to share about issues they would rather not share or to share more about certain things than they wish to. The presentation portion of the assignment is also part of the assessment. Here, we will be making sure that each student actually gives a presentation of about 5 minutes and that the students respond to the questions or thoughts their classmates offer—again, in collegial ways that maintain the presenting student's control over what is shared. One other issue of which we should remain mindful is that because the assignment is intended to build community and to teach class members (including the teacher) important information that can guide future teaching and learning, our assessment should be guided by an appreciative stance that honors students' contributions, rather than a viewpoint that sets out to find what is absent, incomplete, or wrong in the work our students have completed.

> ***Self-portraiture prompt.*** What do you want your classmates and me to know about who you are? This self-portraiture assignment will allow you to do just that. It will also help us notice some things you know and do well, and things you want to keep getting better at, that we can include in the academic work we do in our class. What you share will also help us develop some careful ways of thinking about our cultures, languages, and everyday activities. There are a number of things you can share in your self-portrait:
>
> - The community, city, state, or country in which you were born, and other places in which you and family members have lived or still spend time. What are some important things you know about those places? What are some important ways in which they are similar and different?
> - The different schools you have attended and what was/is enjoyable or hard about being in those schools. You can also pick one or two specific classes that make some important points about your learning experiences in school.
> - The ethnic, racial, or national cultures that are part of who you and your family are. What are some important things you know and learned from being part of those cultures?

- The languages you speak, understand, and write, including any kinds of language that you think are "slang" or casual. Where, when, how much, and with whom do you use them?
- Some of your special interests or activities you enjoy on your own, with family, or friends, and the different places you carry out those activities. Think as broadly as you can—from hanging out with your friends in different community or online spaces; reading and writing, including writing songs, poetry, stories, or your reflections on your life in a special notebook; sharing your writing with others; communicating with others on your cellphone or computer; dancing; making art; and so on. What languages, special tools, or equipment do you use for carrying out these activities?
- You can present your self-portraiture as a piece of writing, such as an autobiographical piece or a story; on a poster board with pictures or examples of things that are important about who you are; or in a PowerPoint or Prezi with links to any spaces you want us to visit online. You can also write and perform (and even video record if you have the time, interest, and technology resources and skills) a short skit or dramatic performance highlighting a significant issue or experience from your life. You can also prepare a talk to give to our class and bring any special items that tell something about who you are. We will spend time discussing what you share with us, and you can choose to share any other details about you that you are comfortable sharing.

One Teacher's Related Instructional Assignments for Learning About Her Students

Heather is an ESL literacy teacher who teaches in the Toronto area in Canada. She had been teaching for 20 years when we met during my study into student diversity and English language arts curriculum. Heather had also taught English to adult new immigrants to Canada before she embarked on a high school English teaching career. As an Anglo, Canadian-born teacher, these adult ESL teaching experiences, combined with extensive travel, facilitated Heather's understandings of, and empathy with, her students' sociolinguistic needs. She explained:

> I had been a fair number of places to put myself in the position of the foreigner or the visitor from another country and experiencing that, the language barrier, and what it's like to try to be learning a new language. And so I have talked to the students about it . . . unless you have experienced that, it is very difficult to put yourself in their position. So, you know, I think for the most part, it has made me very empathetic to their needs.

Heather invented a number of assignments, such as a Coat of Arms and a Poster Project, for learning about her diverse students that achieved a similar goal as the self-portraiture assignment I just described. When I asked Heather what countries her students were coming from, she painted a mosaic teeming with world nations, cultures, and languages. Heather's students hailed from:

> All over . . . there's a boy from Peru. There's a girl from Taiwan, a girl from Poland, a boy from Hong Kong, a couple of boys from China . . . a boy from Korea, and a boy from India, so this class is quite a mix. In my other class, I have a couple of boys from Iraq; girls from Korea; a boy from Nigeria, Africa; a couple of girls from Saudi Arabia; a boy from Brazil; and a boy from Iran, Taiwan, Korea, Iran, again, Pakistan, India . . . another boy from Peru that had an Indian background, actually . . . Pakistan, Korea, and a girl from Germany . . .

Tangible affirmations of cultural diversity were prominently displayed in Heather's classroom. One assignment she used at the beginning of the year was the Coat of Arms. Pointing to her wall in a conversation with me, Heather explained: "We did those coats of arms at the beginning of the year on this wall where they got to talk about their strengths and their weaknesses and their goals, their background, their heritage. . . . We all put on the map where they're from and kept that up. Every time we had a new student to the class they could add their name and show where they're from."

Heather also told me about a Poster Project that achieved the same objective:

> I've often started out [the school year] with a Poster Project where it's just who am I or why am I special and they have to present a poster with their strengths, their weaknesses, their goals, and they have to collect pictures. And some of them have really gone all out. There have been some beautiful posters put together. Some of them have done a PowerPoint presentation. And it's something of course that they . . . know themselves and I think it just really makes them feel good about themselves where they can play up their strengths and tell the class, "You know I used to be a professional." I've got one boy, the boy from Peru, who was a professional horseback rider, or jumper, in his country. So it kind of gives them a chance to boast a bit about their past accomplishments and it helps them to focus on where they're going and what they want to do and how to improve on their weaknesses, what they can do. . . .

Self-portraiture assignments like these are useful for the expansive view they can provide into our students' diverse experiences, knowledge, and language and literacy practices, whether our students are transnational or not. Curricular invitations like these encourage students to bring the transnational and mononational geographies of their lives into school and help us all become transnationally literate.

Critical Questioning of Lived Experience Spanning Local and Transnational Borders

As students paint the landscapes of their lives, they will certainly include issues that deserve critical reflection and further examination. For instance, if Vanesa completed the self-portrait assignment, we can imagine her including her noticings, or observations, of economic disparities between the United States and her hometown in Mexico that produced different degrees of access to public libraries and diverse books, and which further accounted for differences in people's reading practices across these international contexts. We can imagine Vanesa articulating some similarities and differences in education that she experienced across the Mexican and U.S. schools she attended. In the same way, our mononational students who choose to focus their self-portraits on their educational experiences in schools in one country will discover commonalities and differences across different school spaces they have inhabited.

Sticking with this example about self-portraits of schooling, we can guide our transnational and mononational students into critical analysis by asking them questions about the following educational domains and inviting them to hypothesize about why similarities and differences exist across their local and transnational schools:

- Different options for schooling
- Language(s) of instruction
- Cultural demographics and descriptions
- Curricular texts, topics, and emphases across schools and grade levels
- Instructional approaches teachers use and students enjoy
- Typical learning activities and assessments

In our teaching roles, we will encourage students to think and talk about the educational strengths and challenges they notice in each context and how they perform socially and academically under different conditions. We can guide students to take up critical perspectives by asking them to consider, for instance, what social and cultural values or beliefs, educational policies, or economic and historical conditions may account for those curricular and instructional differences. Students can offer valuable insights about teaching and learning that could help us adjust our instructional approaches, perhaps to include some new practices that our students know are beneficial for them. We may also be able to consider whether some instructional strategy or curricular approach a student has experienced in another local or international school context might benefit other students in our classroom.

Transnational as well as mononational students who complete the self-portraiture will signal issues of personal, familial, social, educational, or political significance to them on a local, national, or transnational scale. Valerie Kinloch's (2009) work, for example, offers an exemplary view of young people studying the gentrification of their Harlem community through extensive reading, writing, multimodal composition, and sharing and activism with a number of key audiences such as their classmates, local community members, and university students. We would want to pay careful attention to what all our students are sharing about their lives and help them develop critical questions about those issues. Those questions will serve as the basis for further investigation, through critical inquiry projects, about the issues and concerns they raise. Critical inquiry projects, which we will explore further in the next chapter, allow students to pursue individual and/or collective knowledge and understandings about relevant life topics and foreground the idea that students' lived experiences and concerns are central to curriculum, teaching, and learning.

Researching Languages and Literacies Across Local and Transnational Contexts

Self-portraits and other related assignments invite students to display the whole terrain of who they are. We can also frame inquiries into life, language, and literacy more tightly—for example, by asking students to focus on their language practices across different social contexts of their lives. A useful tool for doing so is a language study chart (see Table 2.1). We can guide students to create such a chart, or provide them with a template (an electronic version would encourage students to write beyond the constraints of a physical page), and explain the purpose of this assignment in a similar fashion as we would describe the self-portraiture:

> For a week or 2, we are going to pay close attention to how we use different languages or styles of speaking in different spaces of our lives. What you notice about your uses of language, and your thoughts, feelings, and questions about what you are noticing, will become part of the academic work we do in our class. We will use what you learn to help us develop some careful ways of thinking about and using our languages in school and in other parts of our lives. As a first step, create a chart that includes several columns:
>
> - In column 1, list all the languages and dialects, including what you might call "slang," that you speak.
> - Add at least three columns for three different social contexts. At least one of the contexts should be a personal or social one, like home or a neighborhood basketball club. At least one of the contexts should be an academic class at our school. Make these social context columns big enough to describe the people and activities involved in them and how you use your languages in those spaces.
> - In your last column, at the end of each day, write some things you noticed, felt, or had questions about related to how you used your languages.

Table 2.1. Language Study Chart

My Languages	Social Context 1 (Home)	Social Context 2 (Workplace)	Social Context 3 (an academic class the student chooses)	Feelings, Questions, Noticings, Thoughts
Dominican-accented English	On the phone with one of my sisters during our 30-minute conversation—short phrases, tone, and inflection.	I pronounced certain words in Dominican-accented English.		I consciously switched to Dominican English with my sister, but I know my Dominican accent shows up in small ways in most of my conversations in other social contexts without me intentionally trying, for instance in the way I pronounce certain words.
African American English (AAE)	At home with my husband and son. In the phone conversation with my sister—some phrases, tone, and inflection.	Exchanged greetings in hallways with African American students who greeted me in AAE. In some moments while teaching my university students I used my tone of voice, inflection, or gesture to make a point in AAE.		I blend all my varieties of English at home with my husband and son. I relax control over my language use and allow my Dominican English and AAE to flow more fully and naturally into my speech.

My Languages	**Social Context 1 (Home)**	**Social Context 2 (Workplace)**	**Social Context 3 (an academic class the student chooses)**	**Feelings, Questions, Noticings, Thoughts**
White American Middle-Class English (WME)	At home with my husband and son. The primary form of English I used in my phone conversation with my sister.	The primary language I spoke while teaching and in meetings. The language I used to write work-related and personal emails.		My conversation with my sister today demonstrates best how I combine all my Englishes to communicate most effectively. My sisters and I use mostly WME when speaking to one another but Dominican and AAE Englishes are always present in our speech. I think WME is a very efficient language for us to communicate in because we have so many years of educational and work experience using that language and we use it almost exclusively all day long at work. There are times when we will fully switch to Dominican English or AAE when we have strong viewpoints or emotions about a topic. We also use Dominican English to connect emotionally with each other through our cultural and family identity.

Students can keep this record going for a week or 2, or even longer if they or you think it is continuing to generate new information. Thinking back to Vanesa, we already identified many kinds and sources of information that she could readily pour into such a recording format, and we can expect that all our students will find much to study and say about their language practices. The chart students create could look something like the one in Table 2.1. We could model for our students how to fill out this chart as I have done below based on the different Englishes I speak at home and in my workplace on a typical workday.

A much longer period of record keeping would help students document change in their language practices and their thinking about those practices over time. This documentation can be accompanied by a language journal in which students do more extended daily writing and reflection on their language practices, making at least one entry a day for the duration of their self-study of language. Giving students a stock prompt like this for maintaining a language journal will help:

> Write about the different languages or the different ways you used language today, at home with family members, in your various classes at school, with various groups of friends, and in one or two other situations. What do you notice about the ways you used language in these different spaces and with different people? What seems significant to you about your language practices today?

Vanesa, as we have learned, was full of observations about the ways she used her languages and shifts in her language practices, and she needed opportunities to reflect and develop critical understandings about the purposes and perspectives driving her language practices. A self-study of language, assisted by the language study chart or journal, would have assisted her in these important explorations.

Students can also collect and analyze artifacts of their language practices. If, for instance, Vanesa was a student in one of our classes, we can imagine her selecting her diary as an artifact of her changing language practices. All of us, whether we are transnational or mononational, or speak one or more official language, possess a diverse linguistic repertoire that we draw from and use to participate in different social contexts and achieve a range of social, academic, professional, and other goals. Thus, student-conducted inquiries into their language practices provide an opportunity for all of us to explore and develop critical understandings and perspectives about uses of, and shifts in, our language repertoires.

Going broader than the individual, we can study language or literacy practices among a group of our students, such as a whole class, or within their homes, communities, or other social contexts that students inhabit. These broader forms of inquiry get both our students and us out into the world to study it. Our students can video-record and take notes and photographs of their observations (see, for example, Kinloch, 2009). They can conduct interviews and focus groups with different individuals and groups of people who are part of the spaces in which they live, audio-recording those conversations and taking detailed notes. Students can also collect and analyze a variety of artifacts that tell something important about their language and literacy practices and contexts of participation. Our transnational students may wish to study language use across the national communities in which they participate. In the same way, mononational students who have moved away from other communities in which they have lived might want to include more distant geographies in those investigations. Students in these situations can use digital technologies to assist their research—for instance, interviewing or surveying people who are farther away via phone, email, Google Hangout, Skype, Survey Monkey, or other mutually available digital technologies.

Such research methods are rigorous and enjoyable academic activities through which we can work with our students to identify and document the different geographies that comprise our lives and the language and literacy practices that are produced and negotiated in those spaces. In terms of academic work products, students can deliver oral presentations on their findings. They can also create research reports. These reports can be written descriptive pieces that include interview, survey, and other kinds of data they have collected. Students' reports can also emphasize multimodality (as with the self-portraiture assignment) by making generous use of photographs, physical artifacts, audio and video, and charts or graphs.

A Teacher and Her Students Conduct a Broad Inquiry into Their Literacy Practices

We can also undertake a broader collaborative research project—for example, an inquiry into the literacy practices of our students and the views that they and others hold about young people's literacy practices. This assignment fosters a classroom community that includes all students who come from diverse cultural and linguistic backgrounds, engage in multiple literacy practices, and lead transnational and mononational lives. To elaborate on this example, I draw from Molly Campbell's 9th-grade literacy classroom in Austin, Texas. This classroom has been assigned the label of a "reading" class, meaning it is for students who did not pass (sometimes on several tries across many school years) the state reading test. We will quickly slough off this misnomer of a label that school administrators have affixed to this classroom and the people in it. Across this book, we will use Molly's classroom as an exemplary site to help us envision the kind of teaching and learning that is possible and necessary with transnational and mononational students who all bring cultural, linguistic, and multiliteracies diversity to our classrooms. Molly's classroom includes transnational students like Vanesa who live in and have strong ties to both Texas and Mexico. Some of her students claim Mexican heritage and identify as Mexican American, but not as transnational. Students like these have varied levels of expertise or identification with Spanish. There are also African American students in this particular class who speak African American English. All the students—notwithstanding their transnational, cultural, or linguistic identifications—engage in multiliteracies practices, many of which are shared among the group.

I documented how Molly and her students began a school year by exploring their literacy practices and coming to understandings about what they and others in their families, communities, and school thought about those literacy practices. Molly began with an in-class activity in which she asked each student to write down forms of literacy on individual sticky notes. Students wrote down all the different ways they used reading and writing in their lives and listed other activities in which they participated, both in and out of school, that they thought might contain literacy. Their lists included practices that ranged from keeping journals in multiple languages and participating in online social networking sites that spanned national boundaries to tagging and tattoos, practices that sometimes signified their national, cultural, and linguistic affiliations.

The class then aggregated their lists onto a poster to develop categories. In this way, Molly and her students noticed commonalities across students' literacy practices as well as individual differences they could discuss, and they moved the sticky notes around to form clusters of related literacy practices. With this physical manipulation of brightly colored squares of paper, students who had unique as well as shared national, cultural, racial, and linguistic backgrounds came together in groups connected by their multiliteracies practices. Just as Heather, the Canadian teacher, had put her students' self-portraits and coats of arms on display, this poster remained on Molly's classroom wall for 6 weeks, during which time she frequently referred to it.

That first class ended with Molly giving students an assignment to continue paying attention to, and writing down in their notebooks, different forms of literacy that they found in their lives. Two days later when the class met, she reviewed the group's findings from their previous discussion and asked the students to "write on a sticky note what you are thinking about this finding literacy everywhere in your lives. Do you think differently about whether you are a reader or writer?" Molly then facilitated discussions where the class examined their findings and came to their own definitions of what could and could not count as literacy. Her intention was for students to realize the broad social nature of literacy and to help them recognize and own that they were already highly literate in many ways that they could draw upon in improving as readers and writers in school.

Taking their inquiry further, the class collaboratively created a list of all the literacy practices they had identified, which now included the items on the sticky notes as well as others such as texting, watching movies, graffiti, music, and reading magazines. They translated these items into a survey with a Likert scale, which asked respondents to rate their level of agreement on a scale of five points ranging from strongly agree to strongly disagree. Students were asked to poll a teacher, another adult, and another student who was not in their reading class about whether they considered each of these forms literacy. The students came back with their survey results and ran their statistical analysis. The results of the poll formed the basis of a class discussion in which students responded to the fact that some adults, including most of the teachers surveyed, did not consider certain literate forms that were important to the students to be literacy at all.

Molly confronted the students with the result that 50% of their teachers "thought the things you think are important and are literacy are not, to them." Asking them to think about this in pairs, she then asked what came up in the conversations. As the discussion continued, Molly, contradicting the comments of some of her teacher colleagues, argued that "All literacy practices are connected, but we need to show how they're connected." Molly thus signaled her intention toward generativity (Ball, 2009) and multiliteracies pedagogy (New London Group, 1996) in devising, along with her students, ways in which to connect the academic literacies they were developing in this class to the literacies at which they were already skilled.

Critical Questioning of Language and Literacy Practices

Molly and her students' conversations illustrate appreciative inquiry into students' literacy practices and critical examination of the literacy practices that are valued in school and society. To ensure that early inquiries into our students' language and literacy practices assist them in developing critical perspectives, we would encourage students to articulate the thoughts and questions that came up for them (which we asked students to attend to and record as part of their data collection) as they studied how they and others use their languages and multiliteracies in different spaces of life. Our lines of questioning and our facilitating of class conversations about students' findings will normalize and encourage students' questioning, critique, and development of critical knowledge and perspectives on language and literacy practice across different lifeworlds both in and outside school. We can pose questions to our students such as:

- What do you see as the benefits of having multiple languages and ways of using those languages?
- Which languages and language practices do you see as most useful for you as a member of your family, in a particular country, in certain social settings, in particular academic spaces of school?
- In what ways do your and your family's language practices portray or differ from the dominant language of the society/societies in which you live?
- In what ways do you notice your teachers, your textbooks, your assignments, and other parts of education including or excluding the different language and literacy knowledge, skills, and interests you have outside school?
- Who are the people and groups that make decisions about the language(s) of schools? About the kinds of literacy practices that students and teachers should work on in schools? Why do these people and groups get to make those decisions?
- How do people and groups who make decisions about education ensure that their decisions are followed? What happens to people who agree with and follow those decisions? What happens to those who do not?
- Who are the people and groups that do not get to participate or have their viewpoints counted in official decisionmaking about schools?
- What are some changes you think are needed in the language and literacy practices of school?

- What are some ways in which you as an individual person/student or a member of a social group (such as your neighborhood community or our classroom community) can advocate for, or make changes to, the language and literacy practices of schools?

Questions about language practices get at language ideologies (Martínez, 2010; Orellana & Reynolds, 2008) that shape individuals', social groups', and institutions' beliefs and practices related to language. Questions about multiple languages and literacies invite critical understandings of mere literacy versus multiliteracies and destabilize notions of a single or most privileged form of language or literacy in an increasingly globalized and diverse world (New London Group, 1996). Questions about the language and literacy practices and policies of schools activate knowledge about the ideologies, processes, and power structures involved in determining official curricular knowledge (Apple, 1979, 1993; Bernstein, 1971). Questions about the possibilities and activities pertaining to change position our students and us as important actors in education and in other domains of life where we engage with languages and literacies (Ball, 2009).

In closing out this section, let's conduct a short review of the methods we just considered for discovering who all of our students are, the resources for learning that they carry with them into literacy classrooms, and how transnationalism manifests in those lives, languages, and literacy practices:

- Self-portraiture, and related assignments such as a Coat of Arms of a student's lived experiences, cultures, languages, and literacies
- A tightly framed inquiry, such as a self-study of a student's language practices using observations, note-taking, collection and analysis of artifacts, and reflective writing
- A broader inquiry that explores the multiple languages or literacies of a class of students or those of people in different spaces of our schools and students' communities, using observations, interviews, and surveys, and assisted by digital tools
- Critical questioning about languages and multiliteracies and issues of social, educational, economic, and other concerns spanning local and transnational contexts

With our growing stock of knowledge about transnationalism from the research we reviewed, as well as our own inquiries into our students' lives, we are now prepared to think deeply about what to do with all this knowledge in relation to the academic knowledge and literacies we are building with our students in the literacy classroom. In the next chapter, we will devote ourselves wholeheartedly to the work of becoming generative teachers (Ball, 2009) who connect our transnational and mononational students' repertoires to the teaching and learning processes and objectives of the academic curriculum.

CHAPTER 3

Connecting Transnationalism to the Literacy Curriculum

This chapter will explore how we can make our literacy curriculum more responsive to the transnational knowledge, experiences, and language and literacy repertoires that our students possess. Because this chapter takes us straight into the heart of schooling, curriculum, teaching, and learning, it is essential that we begin with an analysis of the ideological and political factors and actors that influence how we and our students experience the school curriculum. This discussion is especially important in this time of flourishing student diversity amid increasing curriculum standardization that is tied to high-stakes accountability systems. My goal for us as we think together about curriculum in these times is to recognize the imperative and the *possibilities* for teaching in ways that expand the narrow learning objectives, materials, and processes of standardized curriculum to address the many goals and resources that our diverse students bring to the literacy classroom. After this discussion, we will revisit Molly Campbell's classroom to experience how she and her students successfully met this challenge of teaching to diversity in standardized times. We will examine how Molly and her students drew upon and further strengthened students' transnational, multilingual, and multiliterate repertoires to achieve a host of academic, social, political, and other goals. After we visit and debrief about this classroom, we will explore in greater depth the instructional approaches that Molly used so we can leverage them ourselves in our classrooms to meet the goals we and our students hope to achieve from literacy education.

CURRICULUM AS IDEOLOGICAL, POLITICAL, AND ENACTED

The term *curriculum* is often used to signal the set of learning objectives, instructional materials and approaches, and learning activities and assessments that we engage in literacy classrooms (Smagorinsky, 2008). Curriculum, however, as I just implied above, is an ideologically and politically charged idea and endeavor (Apple, 1979, 1993; Applebee, 1974; Bernstein, 1971; M. Young, 1971). Curriculum is ideological because parents, students, teachers, politicians, and different social groups hold very passionate views about what content, skills, and attitudes children and youths should learn in school. All of these groups want schools and teachers to implement the curriculum they believe is right and good for students. Basil Bernstein (1971), a classical theorist on the sociology of knowledge, spoke about ideological conceptions and divisions of the curriculum into sacred and high-status knowledge on the one hand and profane, low-status knowledge on the other. Sacred, high-status knowledge reflected the apex of a society's abstract, intellectual ideas and cultural capital, and the knowledge of its elite ruling classes. In contrast, low-status knowledge reflected the more everyday diverse community experiences of working-class, and, I have argued (Skerrett, 2010), racially, culturally, and linguistically minoritized students and their teachers. Michael Apple (1979) also defined the official curriculum as the educational knowledge that schools affirm and distribute as "socially legitimate knowledge" (p. 6). This official knowledge is hegemonic in nature because it subverted questions such as "Whose knowledge is it? Who selected it? Why is it organized and taught in this way [and] to this particular group?" (p. 7).

As Apple's (1979) question about grouping students to experience different versions of the curriculum suggests, curriculum is political. Curriculum is political because people and groups in positions of economic, cultural, and linguistic privilege in society use their power to ensure that the curriculum is selected, divided, taught, and assessed in ways that ensure their children—but not the children outside of those economic, cultural, and linguistic groups—will excel in schools. Schools thus serve as certifying and authorizing institutions, allowing already privileged students to inherit the positions of power that are currently occupied by the people in their families and social circles (Apple, 1979, 1993; Bernstein, 1971; M. Young, 1971). Bernstein (1971) forcefully argued that "how a society selects, classifies, distributes, transmits and evaluates the educational knowledge it considers to be public, reflects both the distribution of power and the principles of social control" (p. 202). Like Bernstein (1971), Apple (1979) concluded that there are "linkages between economic and political power and the knowledge made available (and not made available) to students" (p. 7). Furthermore, foundational and more recent research such as Jeannie Oakes's (1987, 2005) portrays how students are selected for and distributed among the different tracks of the academic curriculum according to their race and social class.

Curriculum becomes even more politicized when national and local governments and educational institutions make themselves the primary agents that decide on the content, skills, and dispositions that will make up the curriculum; the instructional methods, texts and materials, and chronology, through which the curriculum will be engaged; and the characteristics of students who will be grouped to experience different versions of the curriculum. More and more, the teaching and learning of curriculum is monitored, enforced, and assessed, and students, teachers, and whole schools are either rewarded or sanctioned depending on the extent to which they maintain fidelity to the curriculum and its goals. In my research into the English curriculum in Massachusetts, United States, and Ontario, Canada (Skerrett, 2009, 2010), I found evidence that state and provincial

English language arts curriculum policy, mostly through subtle references and examples, directed school districts, whole English departments, and individual teachers to select specific novels or genres for particular groups of students (for example, Shakespeare for students in advanced English compared with *To Kill a Mockingbird* for students in lower academic tracks). These curriculum policy directives are ideological in nature because they perpetuate the positioning of the knowledge and experiences of European and upper-class groups as more significant than those of people from poor, working-class, or racially and linguistically minoritized backgrounds. I also found evidence of how schools and teachers were directed to engage in a narrow range of traditional learning activities and assessments, such as the literary analysis essay and grading rubrics. Because the language and structure of academic texts such as the literary analysis essay is based on White and middle-class ways of speaking, and because grading rubrics are tightly linked to those elements of language, the overemphasis of this form of assessment provides an advantage for the students who come from White middle-class homes where this discourse is a naturalized part of family interactions.

Thus, curriculum is ideological and political right down to the local schools, English departments, and individual classrooms in which we and our students teach and learn (Franzak, 2008; Skerrett, 2008; 2012b). In addition to the official school curriculum, Apple (1979) described a curriculum-in-use. This refers to teachers' varied enactments of the official curriculum in their classrooms. Curriculum-in-use is "knowledge filtered through teachers" (Apple, 1979, p. 51) that is "negotiated and transmitted in schools beyond the actual formal 'stuff' of curriculum content" (p. 50). This classroom knowledge is differentially distributed among students according to "categories of normality and deviance" (p. 51) held by teachers about their students and about knowledge. In the English departments she studied, Franzak (2008) found that individual teachers believed—despite not being able to provide evidence to support their convictions—that their department required teachers to teach particular books, or to teach reading using specific methods to students in "reading" classes. Franzak (2008) suggested that teachers' own ideologies and preferences about what English should be about were sometimes responsible for their teaching practices even though they claimed their approaches stemmed from their departments' beliefs and directives.

As English teachers, then, we all have our own perspectives about what English should be about. Our ideological views, and our attendant curricular and instructional preferences, emerge from our own K–12 English education, our subsequent college English majors and other university academic experiences, our broader social and cultural locations and experiences as people in the world, the teacher education programs that prepared us to teach English, and the professional communities we participate in or affiliate with (Siskin, 1994; Skerrett, 2008, 2011). For instance, in my own research into English teachers' enacted curriculum, I discovered that teachers who had personal experiences with diversity and disadvantage and who had been prepared in English education programs where teaching for social justice was emphasized were the most willing and able to innovate and teach English in ways that foregrounded antiracism and social justice. My research findings are promising because they show that when we value the different forms of diversity our students bring to classrooms and develop our professional knowledge and expertise for drawing on these resources for teaching and learning, both we and our students can experience a generative literacy education that meets and exceeds the narrow knowledge and learning goals that comprise official curriculum policies today.

CLASSROOM INTERLUDES: DRAWING ON MULTILITERACIES, MULTILINGUALISM, AND OTHER TRANSNATIONAL RESOURCES FOR LITERACY EDUCATION

Thus far, we have been positioning our students' diversity—their local and global cultural, linguistic, and multiliterate knowledge and capabilities—as high-status knowledge despite the fact that standardized curriculum often relegates them to the category of profane, low-status, and everyday knowledge (Bernstein, 1971). Now, we will explore specific approaches through which we can draw on our students' repertoires of cultures, languages, and literacies for teaching and learning the academic objectives of the literacy curriculum while also expanding the goals of the curriculum to address students' own goals for literacy engagement. Molly Campbell's 9th-grade literacy classroom, which I introduced in the previous chapter, is an educational space where the teacher and her students engage, from appreciative and critical perspectives, their transnational and local cultural knowledge and multiple languages and literacies to develop their academic literacies of reading and writing. As they build academic repertoires, Molly and her students also work to achieve social, personal, and civic literate capacities that are important for them as people in a transnational world.

A brief overview of Molly's curricular and instructional approaches to literacy education will help us better contextualize the observations we are about to make in her classroom. In Molly's class, students select their own books from a classroom library that Molly thoughtfully stocks to reflect students' diverse life experiences, cultures, and language and literacy practices. They read these books independently, in pairs, or in small groups. Students also engage in a variety of forms of daily writing as they read that supports them as they make sense of texts. One form of daily writing is the keeping of journals in which students interact personally with the texts they are reading. This academic practice fosters deep, reflective thinking. Students also share their journal writing with one another, giving their classmates insights into their personalities and thinking processes. Writing on sticky notes is another daily practice students use to support meaning-making. For instance, Molly directs students to find quotes from their books to support the broad themes or ideas they find significant in their reading. Students then jot down quotations and page numbers on sticky notes to assist them with this textual inquiry. All of these daily forms of writing help support Molly's more extensive writing instruction through which students produce lengthier narratives and textual analyses.

Interlude 1. Multiliteracies Resources for Growing as Readers and Writers

Recall from Chapter 2 that Molly and her students have already taught us how to become well versed in our own students' multiliteracies practices. We'll now see Molly and her students engaging their multiliteracies practices authentically as they undertake academic work. In fact, Molly and her students begin the class we're about to observe by talking about the voluminous amounts of texting students do on their cellphones each day, with Molly legitimating this practice as a contributor to students' development as readers and writers.

Molly: You've changed so much in your reading. Now you're underlining stuff and you're scratching your chin and you're underlining some more. . . . I can see the wheels turning. I think that texting has really helped you become better readers.

Darius: I don't text.

Molly: Well, a lot of people text and in my other class we were trying to figure out . . . [To Nina:] Do you have text history on your phone? How many [texts] have you done today?

Nina: 180.

Molly: Only 180?

Diego: Damn!

Molly: These kids, by the end of the day yesterday, two of them had over a thousand texts by the end of the day. And I don't know if they're telling me the truth or not. I assume they are . . .

Nina: That's true.

Molly: [In my other class] they did a text [and] it took 10 seconds. So we figured out if you do a thousand texts a day and they are 10 seconds long that's 2 and a half hours. So that's time you're reading and writing not in school.

Darius (who had left class briefly to check on whether the school nurse's office was open because he was not feeling well) returns and rejoined the conversation, asking, "What are y'all doing? Texting? I can text faster than all of y'all," although he had initially claimed that he does not text. Molly asks Nina to start texting so that they can compute an average of how much she reads and writes each day through this multiliteracies practice. Nina begins texting as Molly keeps time on her stopwatch.

Molly: Thirty seconds . . . so you had 161 texts and they were 30 seconds long . . . it's almost an hour of texting what you did yesterday. You texted for almost an hour.

Nina: Especially when I'm mad, I text so fast.
Molly: So if that's your average you read and write for about an hour a day.
Molly [to the class]: How many of you text for an hour a day? The reason I'm doing this is because I really feel that part of this growth [in your reading] is what you do on the cellphones and the computer . . .
Darius: No other teacher would have thought of that, Miss. You're the only teacher. That's really cool. Most teachers are like "Put your cellphones away!"

Later that class session, as she prepared students for an independent reading session, Molly reminded students to practice the cognitive strategy of envisioning (creating pictures in one mind's of the actions, scenes, characters etc. as one reads a text) to improve their understanding of what they read. "Two things I know you do but you don't write about it much. How does it look in your head? How do you imagine it?" Reminded of students' passion for hip-hop (and knowing that some of them were reading a book about the life of legendary hip-hop artist Biggie Smalls that she had included in the classroom library), Molly connected the cognitive work of envisioning to students' multiliteracies practices. "If you're reading about Biggie Smalls, what does he look like?" she asked the class. This mention of the artist reminded Darius of a movie made about Smalls's life. Darius excitedly asked, "Miss, have you seen *Taken*? That movie's live! That movie's tight!" Molly connected Darius's comments to the skill she was teaching: "So speaking of movies . . . do you see big pictures? Do you see flashes?" [Fieldnotes, 3/31/2010]. Molly's question to Darius about whether he sees big pictures or flashes as he envisions relates to the idea that each individual envisions uniquely—for instance, some people create a moving motion picture in their mind of what is happening in a text; others might create one or more vivid pictures, almost like snapping a photograph.

In this instructional event, then, Molly invited students into the literacy work of the day by privileging their outside-school literate lives and making authentic connections to their digital reading and writing practices on their cellphones and their growth as readers and writers in the literacy classroom. Molly further drew on her students' knowledge of and affinity for hip-hop by referencing a book in their classroom library that some students were reading about the legendary artist Biggie Smalls for teaching and learning the academic objective of the day—the reading strategy of envisioning. It is clear that students' engagement with this strategy for understanding texts was enhanced by their hip-hop-based knowledge and literacy practices. Darius invoked another outside-school literacy that was related to the topic of Biggie Smalls and the class' literacy work of envisioning—watching the movie *Taken*, which features the artist. Thus, when we explicitly acknowledge our students' outside-school multiliteracies practices as valuable forms of literacy engagement that have substantive connections to the learning they are undertaking in school, our students will approach the literacy curriculum with confidence that they are already capable literate people who can only learn and develop more fully by engaging with literacy learning in school.

Interlude 2. Multilingualism and Transnational Experiences for Growing as Readers

The classroom excerpt below, taken from the same class session we just examined above, portrays how students' reading and understanding of texts were assisted by their multilingual and transnational knowledge and capacities.

> Students get up from their desks to choose books from the classroom library. Vanesa, whom you'll recall is a Mexican transnational girl; Nina, another girl who is Mexican American but, like Vanesa, is also transnational; and Darius, a mononational African American boy are all reading the same transnational story, *Sold.* The text is an award-winning novel by Patricia McCormick (1996) about a young girl from rural Nepal who is sold into sexual slavery in India and endures and survives its horrors. The young woman teaches herself to speak and read English in the multilingual, transcultural space of the brothel, and eventually escapes with the help of an American man.
>
> Vanesa and Nina begin their conversation in Spanish as they walk over to the classroom library shelves. Nina walks over to Vanesa's desk, looks over Vanesa's journal entry, and exclaims, "Man! Yours is long!" and laughs. Vanesa asks her, "Want to hear it?" to which Nina answers, "Yes." Vanesa begins reading her journal to Nina, who listens. I listen in too as Vanesa reads to Nina: "A woman is thinking about getting work but she doesn't know what her real job is [will be]." Shortly thereafter, Nina asks Molly, "Can we [Nina and Vanesa] read together? Outside [meaning in the hallway outside the classroom door, a favorite spot for students to read]?" Molly responds, "Start quietly first [inside the classroom]." Nina looks at her and responds, a bit mockingly, "I'll do it. For you." She pulls her chair closer to Vanesa and they begin reading together. A few minutes later, Vanesa bursts out, "Ewww!" Molly relents, "Shhh!! Okay. Go outside." The girls jump up as Vanesa exclaims to Nina about their book: "This is good!" Nina responds, "Oh my God!"
>
> Molly steps outside 7 minutes later to check on the girls and finds Darius (whom Molly had allowed to go back to the nurse's office, as it was not open when he had first tried to visit), standing outside with them.
>
> *Molly:* Darius, what are you doing?"
> *Darius:* [Inaudible, but something along the lines of he's also reading that book]
> *Molly:* Then go get a book.
> *Darius:* I was!
> *Molly:* Get your own book. And get a sticky note.
> *Darius:* Where they at?
> *Molly:* Here, babe.
> *Darius:* I like this book.

Molly: Do you want a sticky note?
Darius: Yeah. I'm gonna fill this sticky note up!
Molly laughs.

Several minutes later, Nina, Vanesa, and Darius re-enter the classroom. Nina and Vanesa talk briefly to each other in Spanish.

Nina [very animatedly and excitedly]: I can see it! It reminds me of the movie *Taken*!
Molly: Write that.
Vanesa: [not fully clear] . . . a picture.
Nina: Okay. Wait. That I can see it?
Molly: Yes, how you see it is different from how I see it?
Nina and Vanesa talk briefly to each other in Spanish.
Darius: So you're supposed to write . . . so can I put like . . . so I want to write about when she can't dream no more.
Molly: That's sad, right? Write . . .
Darius: I want to write how she's been harassed to the point she can't dream no more.
Vanesa and Nina are talking excitedly to each other in English and Spanish.
Vanesa: I like that movie. *Me gusta mucho*. Yes, when the dog died. [Fieldnotes, 3/31/2010]

This classroom excerpt shows how students' language practices were welcomed in this classroom, just like their multiliteracies practices, and served as teaching and learning tools. Students like Vanesa and Nina used Spanish to understand and analyze their books, which were written in English. Darius spoke his home language to his teachers and peers as he conducted high-quality academic work with his transnational peers. Indeed, the book that Vanesa, Nina, and Darius came together to read was a transnational tale and thus further enhanced the transnational character of the classroom. It is easy to understand why transnational students were drawn to the transnational literature Molly included in the classroom library, and it is also clear that Darius, though he did not claim a transnational lifestyle himself, was deeply moved by the text. The animated responses of all three students as they returned to the classroom to write and share with their teacher about their interactions around the text suggested the richness of the literacy experience they shared in around this transnational story.

Interlude 3. Transnationalism Expanding the Goals of the Literacy Curriculum

As part of her professional stance, Molly listened carefully to her students to learn about the everyday issues on their minds that were not necessarily captured in the curriculum. As a generative teacher, she was continuously innovating ways to make the curriculum responsive to the interests, concerns, and needs of her students. This last interlude of classroom life shows how the entire school context—not just Molly's classroom—was a transnational space as Vanesa shares about a boy from Haiti who is a new arrival to their school. A closely related note to bear in mind is that this class session occurred on March 31, 2010; we'll hear students reference the devastating earthquake that Haiti had suffered a few weeks earlier, on January 12.

Vanesa: Oh, Miss! There's a boy from Haiti!
Nina: Oh! Yes!
Darius: Is he Black?
Students laugh.
Darius [teasing the girls]: Is he tall?
José: Oh my God! [In a mock girly tone]
Darius [continuing the teasing]: Is he hot?
Vanesa: He doesn't know . . . like nothing.
Darius: English?
Vanesa: He speaks French but I can speak to him [Recall from Chapter 1 that Vanesa has been taking French as an elective.]
Molly: That's so exciting!
Nina: [Looks up at the clock on the classroom's front wall] Sí . . . [agreeing with Molly that the Haitian youth's arrival at their school is exciting].

Nina's upward glance is my cue that class is about to end. She tells Molly not to forget to show me the video. Nina is referring to the new music video, a version of the "We Are the World" song that a number of the students' favorite artists had performed together to assist disaster relief efforts in Haiti. I know that the students have already watched the video twice in class, both times when I was absent. Nina had also told Molly a number of times before this class visit of mine that the class needs to show me the video. Nina retrieves Molly's laptop from Molly's desk in a corner of the classroom. It takes a while to pull up the video on the Internet and Nina begins to get anxious, saying, "Now we won't have time to see it." The video begins to play. Nina turns to me, saying, "Miss! They say that [hip-hop artist] Fifty Cent is in it but halfway in. And it's about 8 minutes long and the bell's about to ring." Darius seems to have not seen the video before either, because he asks his classmates, "When did you all see it?" José responds, "Like twice. In here." Nina insists, "They need to see it. Especially her [pointing to me]." We get to watch about 3 minutes of the video before the bell rings. The students start running off. I say "Bye, guys," and keep watching the video. Vanesa says, "I'll stay," but then leaves seconds later, also needing to get to her next class.

After I finish watching the video, Molly tells me that the students have become very interested in the situation in Haiti. She informs me that Nina came across the video outside of school and told the class they should all

> watch it together. Molly says she'd like for the class to put together some school supplies to send to children in Haiti. She adds, "I've always wanted to do a social justice unit and maybe they can do that [on Haiti]." Thinking of her upcoming writing unit on memoir, Molly adds, "Maybe I'll give them a choice. That they can either do their memoir or write something about Haiti, why it's so important to them." [Fieldnotes, 3/31/2010]

Transnationalism, once more, entered the classroom space naturally in this single period when Vanesa mentions the boy from Haiti joining one of her classes and how she is able to speak with him in French. As the interactions at the end of the period suggest, the students had had Haiti on their minds for some time now—they wanted to participate in the global conversation and response to the devastation of an already ravaged country in their world. As Molly and I talked about teaching at the end of the period, she displayed generativity by beginning to think about how an upcoming unit on memoir—one that is already open to transnational experiences (as you will later see in some of the texts that students produced)—can be made even more transnationally inviting by expressly welcoming students to write about why Haiti is important to them. Furthermore, Molly began to think about designing a social justice unit in which students could conduct critical inquiry about the situation in Haiti and link those events to a broader project on social justice in the world.

INSTRUCTIONAL APPROACHES TO FOREGROUND TRANSNATIONALISM IN THE LITERACY CURRICULUM

The approaches to teaching and learning highlighted in the classroom interludes above suggest some key ways in which we can connect transnationalism to the literacy curriculum. We will now further explore and expand upon these approaches, which include:

- Selecting diverse texts that draw upon, and further build, students' transnational and multicultural knowledge and consciousness, multiliteracies, and multilingual repertoires
- Reading and writing in ways that recruit and strengthen those transnational, multicultural, multilingual, and multiliteracies repertoires
- Conducting critical inquiry into the texts students read and write as well as into broader issues that interest and concern students, including those of a transnational character

One additional approach I will offer is a set of generative questions that we can ask ourselves across the different seasons of our curriculum so that we can continuously orient ourselves to teach responsively to transnationalism as part of our educational stance and daily practices.

Selecting Diverse Texts

The curricular texts that enter diverse classrooms should honor and build students' multiple cultures, languages, and literacies. We can offer students a variety of texts that reflect their cultural worlds and the languages of their homes and communities (Ball, Skerrett, & Martínez, 2010). In keeping with the multiliteracies tradition (New London Group, 1996), we would also add texts that portray the literacy affinity groups to which our students belong (videogamers, sports enthusiasts, fashionistas) to our classroom library shelves. From the knowledge she gleaned from early inquiries into students' language and multiliteracies practices (as we saw in Chapter 2) Molly created, and regularly updated, a classroom library stocked with diverse genres on a range of relevant topics from which students could choose. Here are some of the kinds of texts that were included in Molly's classroom library:

- Teen romances set in urban communities
- Graphic novels and cartoons that reflected the TV shows students watched
- Transnational and transcultural stories
- Poetry anthologies, including rap
- Biographies of rappers, historical figures, and athletes students admired
- Science fiction
- Newspapers and current event articles including those on the Internet
- Low rider and sports magazines

Several of the books in the classroom library were written in Spanish and African American English, the other primary languages Molly's students spoke, and many of the texts contained code-switching and other language practices that the students used. When they used the Internet to read during class, Spanish-speaking students often gravitated to sites maintained in Spanish.

To foreground transnationalism in our curricular texts, we should be mindful of selecting stories, news articles, or other informational texts about border crossing across different national geographies and texts that explore the particular social, familial, cultural, economic, linguistic, educational, and other issues that arise for transnational people. As we welcome students from different national, linguistic, and cultural backgrounds into our classrooms and find out about their literate lives and interests, we can add texts to our classroom library that reflect our students' growing diversity. Relating border crossing to all of our students' lives, we can carefully select novels and other texts that treat the theme of border crossings of all kinds—cultural, linguistic, social, religious, gender, political, and more that occur within national geographic boundaries and for mononational people. Students have a history of reading texts in the Eurocentric canon, and some of these texts will likely be included in our curriculum, but they should neither dominate the curriculum nor be positioned as having higher value than the texts that reflect students' lives. Re-envisioning curricular texts to foreground our students' national and cultural ties, languages, and literacies requires critical framing (New London Group, 1996) and ideological work (Ball, 2009) on our part and on the part of our students.

Reading Across National, Cultural, Linguistic, and Multiliteracies Borders

We want to give our students ample opportunities to read independently in their areas of interests but to also interact with their classmates within and across national, cultural, language, and literacy affinity groups. Reading across these borders stretches students' knowledge about one another, the worlds in which they live, and how many kinds of texts can represent those worlds. The textual interactions we observed in Molly's classroom among Nina and Vanesa—Mexican and Mexican American transnational youths—and Darius, an African American mononational youth, illustrate the potential of reading across transnational, cultural, linguistic, and multiliteracies borders. The text *Sold* itself was a piece of transnational literature that the three students had chosen and had come together to read. The two transnational youths who shared national, linguistic, and cultural backgrounds conducted a significant portion of their academic conversation in English and Spanish, and we can imagine how their own lived experiences of transnationalism and border crossing assisted their engagement with and understanding of this text.

The African American member of the group also used his home language to collaborate with his peers in this work, and the transnational students' perspectives and experiences thus also became available to him, and vice versa, in their individual and collaborative meaning-making enterprises. Rather than viewing Nina and Vanesa's interactions in Spanish as a practice that excluded Darius, who was not a speaker of Spanish, we can critically reframe this situation as a learning opportunity in which a monolingual student gained an experiential view of the academic benefits of owning additional languages that are sometimes dismissed by the official curriculum. Darius's own diversity as a speaker of different Englishes provided a point of linguistic understanding and appreciation among the three classmates. Furthermore, as all three students worked on their processes of envisioning, they kept in mind how they engaged this cognitive process in an outside-school literacy and an art form that they all knew and valued—a movie featuring a hip-hop artist they all admired. Thus, the daily academic work of reading in this classroom contained a transnational, multicultural, multilingual, and multiliterate character as the teacher and the students drew upon all of their repertoires in the normal course of teaching and learning.

Below are some approaches we can take to reading within and across borders with our diverse students (see Bomer, 2011, for a comprehensive treatment of teaching and learning approaches to reading and writing in language arts classrooms):

- Independent reading units in which individual students read in the areas of their unique interests provide them with opportunities to recruit and strengthen their special language and literacy practices or cultural knowledge through literacy work in school. A transnational student would enjoy opportunities to read fiction, informational, or other texts about one or more of the countries to which he or she has ties.

- Book clubs provide opportunities for students to have a shared text experience on a topic of common interest. Bringing students together around shared interests in a book club—such as what occurred among Vanesa, Nina, and Darius—is one way for students to have social and academic interactions and build relationships across transnational, cultural, and linguistic diversity. The diversity of experiences and perspectives that come together, even in small partnerships, creates opportunities for students to develop ways of negotiating across and learning productively from difference, and adds to their cultural and linguistic knowledge and repertoires.
- Reading partnerships or book clubs that allow students who have shared home language and cultural backgrounds to read and talk about texts together foster their cultural and linguistic repertoires in schools. A reading partnership or book club will also work well for two or more transnational students to engage about living transnationally.
- Whole-class text experiences at different points across a year allow diverse experiences, perspectives, and ways of speaking, knowing, and understanding the world and texts to combine for complex textual experiences. One way to raise transnational awareness is to select a text for a whole-class experience (meaning a novel, short story, poetry, or feature article) that introduces a transnational phenomenon. Whole-class readings and discussions of transnational texts create opportunities for all students to develop knowledge and perspectives about transnational issues, cultural flexibility, and global awareness.
- Another way to teach and learn about border crossing is to select a text for whole-class reading and discussion that emphasizes the phenomenon of border crossing from a nongeographical perspective—for example, crossing racial, social class, or religious borders within one national context. This kind of textual experience will develop students' awareness of how we all cross borders in our everyday lives and will help students identify and value the skills and capacities that are needed for successful border crossing.

Critical Inquiry into the Texts We Read

Diverse texts bring new worlds, experiences, and perspectives into the literacy classroom while allowing us to engage with the literary tools and processes we apply to the traditional literature that often overwhelms the official curriculum (Lee, 2007). For instance, as they read transnational literature and hip-hop biographies, Molly and her students engaged in academic literacy work such as envisioning, reflecting, finding textual evidence, and conducting literary analyses. When we bring diverse text forms together in a classroom, we do much more than just value students' cultures, languages, and literacy practices. We create unique and powerful learning conditions for students to access critical forms of knowledge and understanding that are not typically available to them when teaching and learning emphasize traditional texts that feature a dominant nation, culture, language, and semiotic (meaning alphabetic print) form. Reading diverse text forms helps us and our students notice shared and distinctive design elements (New London Group, 1996) within and across the texts we read. These design elements may take the forms of semiotic tools such as language and visual signs (or multimodal designs like those found in graphic novels), and social or cultural lifeworlds and experiences (such as transnational experiences).

We will be developing a metalanguage of design with our students (New London Group, 1996) as we notice and discuss similar and different design elements and ways of using them across diverse texts. This metalanguage of design is a deep understanding of how authors strategically use diverse meaning-making tools, such as life experiences and language variety, in crafting literary works. This knowledge is critical because it allows us and our students to draw parallels and distinctions among many kinds of texts and notice and critique the underlying ideologies about high- and low-status cultural and linguistic knowledge that influence how texts are selected for school (Apple, 1979, 1993; Bernstein, 1971; Lee, 2007). Through such questioning, we will become more aware of the values and beliefs about different nations, cultures, lifestyles, languages, and literacy practices that shape curriculum policy decisions in relation to literary texts. In a recursive manner, such academic learning will promote, using Ball's (2009) concepts of teachers' generativity, our and our students' ideological becoming and internalized stances that diversity in its many instantiations in texts and in life supports students' academic development. In relation to the literature curriculum, we and our students will further strengthen our agency and capacity to create our own definitions of what constitutes a high-quality text and reading experience for ourselves.

Figure 3.1 provides some instructional activities with which we can guide our students into obtaining these kinds of critical knowledge and understandings about curricular texts.

Writing Across National, Cultural, Linguistic, and Multiliteracies Borders

Transnationalism can support teaching and learning the many forms of writing that are part of literacy curricula—from the daily writing students conduct on sticky notes, in journals, and in reader's and writer's notebooks to lengthier forms of writing they undertake. As they draw on their cultural, linguistic, and multimodal repertoires for writing in school, transnationalism will also emerge as a resource for academic writing. In the second classroom interlude above, I showed how transnationalism, in conjunction with other resources students bring to school, supported daily writing in Molly's classroom. What is important to

Figure 3.1. Developing Critical Perspectives on the Literature Curriculum

- Every 6 to 9 weeks, create a list of the texts students have read during that time.
- Make a chart using these categories (and others that you and your students think are pertinent) to compare and contrast the texts: genre, time period (when the texts were written, as well as when the story is set), nations and cultures represented (of the author and in the work), language(s) of and in the text, and basic storyline or content.
- In writing, have students reflect individually (and/or in partnered, small-group, and whole-class discussions) on the parallels and distinctions they notice among these texts.
- Create partnerships or groups of students who have read texts representing different national, cultural, and linguistic backgrounds, time periods, and genres (perhaps also include a canonical text that the class has read together if your department insists that all students read a specific text from the canon). Have students discuss what they have noticed about how authors use life experiences, culture, and language and other design elements as tools in crafting literary works.
- Invite students to share their thinking about the value, importance, or success of the various texts their group members or the whole class have read and why they think the way they do.

remember about these forms of daily writing is that Molly and her students engaged these writing practices with and across diverse texts, including transnational works. Returning to Molly's classroom will help us examine more fully how transnationalism can serve as a resource for more in-depth writing instruction that leads to extended composition.

One substantial composition unit that Molly and her students undertook was memoir writing. This writing unit entailed an intensive 6 weeks of instruction. Molly began by directing her students to return to their earlier writing as possible sources of inspiration for the lengthy pieces they would be composing. The unit included numerous mini-lessons on topics such as word choice, audience, dialogue, imagery, punctuation, and characterization, and students engaged in multiple revisions of their texts along the way. The end product was a class magazine to which each student and the teacher contributed a polished memoir, and a class celebration where each author read his or her work aloud and engaged in conversation with the class about it. Students received their own copies of the class magazine so they could share their work with other audiences, such as parents, friends, or the larger local or global community—anyone they felt needed to experience them.

In this unit, Molly and her students drew upon students' transnational repertoires (and, concomitantly, their multilingual and multiliteracies repertoires) as resources for developing and displaying academic literacies in writing. For example, here is Molly teaching students how to use dialogue:

> Molly asks Kandace [an African American student] for permission to use her story again. Molly reads from Kandace's text. "Where's your momma at?" Molly stops reading and says to the class: "What did I just say? When a new person talks, new paragraph. . . ." Nina repeats, "Where your momma at?" and giggles a bit at hearing Molly speaking a partial African American English (AAE), without the full intonation or grammar of an AAE speaker. [Fieldnotes, 12/01/2009]

Because Molly invited and legitimized students' entire linguistic repertoires in the academic and social life of the classroom, her students drew upon their diverse linguistic tools as they composed academic texts. One student, Lydia, after the mini-lesson described in part above, began writing using the local conventions of texting that the students in this school community had invented. Unsure about whether Molly would prefer that Lydia use a more official and school-like register and orthography, I queried Molly after class. Molly answered that Lydia's choices were appropriate, especially because Lydia had, up until now, put nothing down for her new draft of the memoir assignment. Molly emphasized that Lydia was *writing*, which was the academic objective. Thus, she accepted students' writing in all sorts of conditions. . . . Molly said to me, "It's just celebrate, celebrate, celebrate, look at your story, look how good your story is." [Fieldnotes, 12/01/2009]

Across my classroom observations during the memoir writing unit, I noticed that students' as well as the teacher's authorial decisions frequently involved language, including when or how much to use Spanish or English in their compositions. Molly titled one of her own compositions for the class magazine "Dar La Luz," "giving the light," a Spanish expression for giving birth. She explained to her students, "I liked that expression. I think it sounds really pretty in Spanish so I picked it." In one conversation, Vanesa explained to me that, for the transnational story "Dad & Me" she was writing, she was considering either including a letter from her mother in the United States to her father in Mexico in a conventional narrative or using that letter as the basis of the story itself. In an earlier conversation she had had with Molly, they had discussed the possibilities of either including the whole letter or else summarizing it. As Vanesa worried over her options and the benefits of each, she reasoned, "It's in Spanish, so I would have to translate it."

While writing for the magazine during the second semester, Nina, who was attempting onomatopoeia in her story that was set in the United States–Mexico border town where she was born, asked Molly, "How do roosters sound?" Molly responded, "Well, roosters say cock-a-doodle-do. Chickens cluck or they squawk. What do roosters say in Spanish?" In response to Nina's and Vanesa's (who was sitting nearby) laughter, Molly insisted, "Different animals say different sounds in Spanish." She asked Vanesa, "What sounds do dogs make [in Spanish]?" to which Vanesa, answered "Wow, wow, wow." "Wow, wow, wow," repeated Molly. "In English, they say bow." [Fieldnotes, 4/21/2010]. In small ways like this, as well as in larger curricular moves, Molly legitimated, and asked students to capitalize on, their existing transnational knowledge, experiences, and languages.

When the students' compositions were completed, Molly compiled their pieces, students designed the magazine cover, and they held a class party that Molly called a "campfire reading"—she placed a lamp in the center of the room and everyone sat around it. There, each student and the teacher shared a story from his or her life. Because some of these stories were multilingual tales, language brokering was an important dimension of sharing texts. During the first semester's class magazine celebration, for instance, Carlos, a recent immigrant from central Columbia, after sharing his story, explained what his dad was like in Spanish to Nina and Angelica, who were translating for Molly. Molly, wanting to be sure she understood, asked Carlos, "He read books to you? No? Oh, you read books to him! Oh, now I'm gonna cry." [Fieldnotes, 12/11/09] Below are two transnational stories, one produced by Nina, the other by Vanesa, the result of 6 weeks of academic work in this classroom. The images of Nina's and Vanesa's stories (Figures 3.2 and 3.3, respectively) presented below are the original versions of their texts; however, in Nina's story you will notice some blank spaces in the text which indicate that I have removed the real names of people and places Nina mentioned in her narrative.

Critical Inquiry into Our Composing Processes

Our writing instruction, like Molly's practice, will need to be informed by a critical stance that recognizes and relies upon students' cultural, linguistic, and multiliterate repertoires as assets for teaching and learning. Molly's daily whole-class instruction, such as the mini-lessons on language and elements of the target genre, her individual conferences with students as they composed, and student-to-student as well as whole-class intellectual interactions around their developing and completed compositions demonstrate for us how to enact a critical approach in writing instruction. The processes in which students engaged to produce their texts also became subjects of critical inquiry in Molly's approach to teaching composition (Canagarajah, 2006). Critical inquiry into our students' writing processes represents a form of overt instruction that encourages our own and our students' metacognitive awareness of students' cultural, language, and literacy strengths and how they and we are thinking about and using these strengths to develop academic literacies (Ball, 2009; New London Group, 1996).

When we regularly ask our students to talk about the texts they compose (not just the texts other authors have written), students become more adept at thinking through and making explicit to themselves, to us, and to their peers the intentions behind the composition moves they made, the particular strategies they employed to carry out their designs, and what they perceive as the effects of their language and literacy choices on their texts and their audiences. Our students will further develop the full range of their cultural, linguistic, and literacy repertoires, and become more expert at using these resources productively for academic development. We can use questions like these (on page 60) to facilitate our and our students' critical knowledge and perspectives on their composition processes and texts:

Figure 3.2 Nina's Memoir. "Guela Gallinas."

I was the only one that called her "Guela Gallinas". The reason for it, is because at he r house she had a lot of roosters. Always running around the yard. My cousins and I would always chase them in circles where her garden was. We were in our 4-6, My younger cousin was 4, I was 5, and my cousin was 6 or 7. Since our roosters had long feathered tails my cousins would always try to grab them by their tails, and the chickens would always cackle and jump up a little.

She was really into GOD, and that would make me look up to her. That's the most important thing about her, she was in GODs hands. As I grew up I would go to church with my aunt, she's also named I was named after her. Me, my sister, my mom, my aunt, and her kids would go to church together. I loved going because the music was beautiful everybody would dance and me and my cousins would hold hands and start dancing all together. My great grandma was the reason for me being in church up to today. Sometimes "Guela Gallinas" would read the bible to me when I was a little girl. I remember when she would tell me in spanish "Hay un senor que se llama Jesucristo que te quiere mucho y el es muy bueno". Man, that made me think maybe I can be happy as well with me being in GODs path.

Everything went well; years past by. Our family would visit my grandma in the Valley everytime we had a chance. Until one day we heard that my grandma was in the hospital. I'm not sure where I was when my mom had told me that "Guela Gallinas" was in the hospital. I think that I was in school. Well that weekend we went to the hospital. Our whole family was there. Me, my mom, and my sister walked fast through the white walls of the hospital going up to the 3rd floor, doctors walking all over the place back and forth.

My mom had asked the nurse "What room is " the nurse responded and pointed at the room. We walked in there and just looked at her. My mom started crying, and me and my sister just started crying as well. Guela looked like if she was in pain with all those machine around her and including the oxygen machine on her. She didn't look to comfortable. And she couldn't move a single muscle in her body. She couldn't talk, move, or even open her eyes. All we got from her was breathing in and out.

Next thing my grandpa walks in really quietly and is very speechless. I remember him talking to her telling her in spanish "Ama' estoy aqui. Me escuchas? Levantate porfavor" He gave her a kiss on her forhead and he decided to step out the room. Me and my older sister walked up to her bed again and we were holding her hands. My sister had tears running down her cheeks as she sees my grandma's nails. She grins a little at my mom and tells her "Mira todavia tiene sus unas rositas pintadas cuando se las ise." She kisses her hand and she puts her hand back down by her side. When I was holding her hand, her hand was so warm like if she had a fever. It was a long night, we didn't go home till later.

She was already dead. We found out that it was a machine that kept her breathing. Well I would talk about the funeral but sadly I didn't get to go to my own grandmother's funeral. My mom had told me that I had to go to school. Mainly because it happened back where I was born in .

Guela Maria was a loving person, she means so much to me. What I really loved about her was that she was always in GOD's path and now that she's up there with him. Man she lived a good life with our family. She loved us very much she never showed us bad examples. That's probably why I miss her so much, but not just me our whole family. Up to this day I feel like she's still here sometimes. Sometimes I can feel her watching over me and my family. She'll always be in my heart and memories.

Figure 3.3 Vanesa's Memoir, "Dad & Me."

~! Dad & Me... !!! ♡

I felt I was going to die. Time was the way to wait better. We just need it to wait. My legs, back, hurts, everything was quiet. I wanna scream I just wanna sleep forget everything! Just be in peace. The doc said I had to rest for one week.

I was crying my mom noticed me.

Mom: What's wrong?

Me: Nothing

Mom: No one cries for nothing.

Me: I just feel really bad.

Mom: I don't want to see uu this way! Ur going to be good! Don't worry!

Me:

I believe her for a moment. My dad called. Me with my dad on the phone! My tears fell and fell. I try to stop! I hold the phone with two hands.

Dad: hey girl what's wrong?!

Me: nothing I'm just not good! I felt that is the end.

Dad: Nothing is going to happen! There is nothing to worry about! I don't wanna see uu like that!! I have a strong daughter don't I? Yes I do! You are going to be alright we just need time! Be strong and always remember that we love uu! No matter what happen we love uu!

I breathe...

Me: thanks dad!

His words make me stronger. He makes me feel alive! The fact that my dad is not with us.. It's hard for me but I know he is making a sacrifice for me for us to be better persons and to be prepare for the future but soon we will be together again! Very soon!

Me: I love you too dad!

- What are/were your goals or purposes for composing this text?
- What resources or tools do you need/did you use to produce this text—both material (such as mentor texts, electronic screen, or physical paper) and social or intellectual (personal experiences, cultural knowledge, language practices, literacy practices, conversations with others)?
- What are/were some moments in your composing process where you strategically used your knowledge and skills with language, culture, and multiliteracies to achieve something important in your text?
- In what ways does your completed composition demonstrate your successful use of cultural, linguistic, and multiliteracies knowledge and practices to achieve your intended goals? Point us to some portions in your text that you are especially proud of.
- Who is/are the intended audience(s) for your work? How do you plan on sharing your work with them? What response do you hope to achieve?

Critical Analysis of the Academic Texts Students Compose

Our students' compositions will travel beyond our classroom doors; thus, both they and we would want to become increasingly skilled in understanding and talking with others about the cultural, language, and literacy resources that students possess and are using for academic learning. This capacity to articulate the sophistication and strengths of students' work is especially important in educational climates that are quick to dismiss teachers' and students' knowledge and expertise and sweep students' diversity under the monotone carpet of standardization. Returning to Nina's and Vanesa's memoirs that we read above (Figures 3.2 and 3.3), I will model an analytic exercise through which we can read, understand, and talk with others about students' writing in ways that identify and value the sophisticated nature of their compositions.

Nina's memoir. Nina's memoir (Figure 3.2) was a multilingual composition about the life, death, and legacy of her *abuela* (grandmother—more specifically, her great-grandmother). Its opening scene was set in her grandmother's home in the Rio Grande Valley, the literal borderlands of Texas. Nina began her memoir with the lyrical lines, "I was the only one that called her 'Guela Gallinas.'" In a sophisticated manner that privileged her home language and the familial ties bound up within it, Nina provided an opportunity for those who do not understand Spanish to grasp the meaning behind this special name with which she had graced her great-grandmother. The sentence that followed this opening line read, "The reason for it, is because at her house she had a lot of roosters. Always running around the yard." Nina's next authorial move illuminated a significant part of who she is—her religious identity—and attributed that subjectivity to her great-grandmother's legacy. She drew on the multilingual academic space of her classroom, first using her texting conventions to capitalize the word *GOD* to signal the importance of religion to her great-grandmother, and, by extension, to herself, and then she moved into Spanish to signal the linguistic orientation of her borderland hometown, family, and religious identity. Nina described how, on her family's frequent visits to the borderlands, her great-grandmother read the Bible to her and "would tell me in Spanish '*Hay un senor que se llama Jesucristo que te quiere mucho y el es muy bueno.*'" [There is a man named Jesus Christ who loves you very much and he is very good.] Nina added, "Man, that made me think maybe I can be happy as well with me being in GODs path."

In the next paragraph, with authorial intention, Nina strode quickly across the years to the scene of her great-grandmother's death, with the entire extended family gathered in a hospital room. She demonstrated her family's dexterous linguistic border crossings in an institutional space, with her mother speaking to the nurses in English, but the family addressing one another in Spanish. Nina invited us, her readers, into a special moment of intimacy between her great-grandparents, with her great-grandfather speaking tenderly to her great-grandmother in Spanish, asking her to please wake up. It is important to notice that Nina's written use of Spanish further identified her as a border crosser between that language and English; she wrote in Spanish cued by the syntactical structure of English and the phonology and familial and local conventions of the everyday, spoken version of Spanish that she and her family speak. It is further highly significant that nowhere in her text did Nina translate any Spanish utterances into English, turning on its head the privileging of English that is common every day in school. Nina's linguistic choices, instead, excluded monolingual English readers, while, in an implicitly critical reframing, brought users of Spanish inside the normalized world of her text, and positioned all her readers as Spanish readers (even though they were not). Nina was also aware, because of the organization of this literacy curriculum, that she would share her published composition with her peers, and that in the "campfire reading," she and other Spanish-speaking peers would have opportunities to translate the Spanish portions of her text for her English-only-speaking peers.

This linguistic hybridity, and Nina's structuring of relative privilege in her text, underscore Canagarajah's (2006) point that code meshing is a political act. In another political composition move, Nina ended her narrative with a direct address to her readers: "Well I would talk about the funeral but sadly I didn't get to go to my own grandmother's funeral. My mom had told me that I had to go to school. Mainly because it happened back where I was born." Here, Nina levied a critique of the emotional cost to families whose lives are lived across borders (Gutiérrez, 2008). Nina judged her educational life in Austin, Texas, as the cause for her missing her beloved Guela Gallinas's funeral. Yet her point that her grandmother "was already dead" that last night they spent with her at the hospital strategically defused the power of the emotional blow dealt to her and her family by the educational, and likely, economic, exigencies that required them to return to their lives away from the borderland.

Finally, in ending her memoir, Nina invoked for her readers additional kinds of borders that she and others experience and can navigate—for instance, those between life and death, heaven and Earth. She shared her conviction that her Guela continues to be here on Earth with her, carried in her heart and memories, even as Guela exists in heaven watching over her. Beyond her religious orientation, this belief of Nina's also signified her traditional Mexican culture that blurs the lines between the spirit world, or the world of the dead, and that of the living. Accordingly, Nina used her religious and cultural knowledge to assist her narrative's resolution in a liminal space, not completely heaven or Earth, not simply past, present, or future.

Vanesa's memoir. Vanesa's transnational narrative "Dad & Me" (Figure 3.3) involved the relationship she shared with her father across the United States–Mexico border. In this composition, Vanesa recounted an experience she had when she had been seriously ill while in the United States. In bed and crying, Vanesa was not consoled by her mom's efforts to comfort her. It was a call from her father, in Mexico, that finally reassured Vanesa that she would recover and that encouraged her to be strong.

Vanesa, like Nina, situated her text, which already contained transnational borders, at another borderland in her semiotic choices. She infused the narrative with her artistic identity and multiliteracies practice (New London Group, 1996), appropriating, if modestly, this writing assignment as an opportunity to make a visual text at the margins, liberally decorating and occupying the borders of her composition page. Vanesa further borrowed from a Spanish punctuation practice, placing the exclamation mark at the beginning and end of the story's title (though without the inverted opening exclamation mark that is conventional in Spanish), and the tildes at the beginning and end of the title resemble the mark over the letter *n* that alters the phoneme in Spanish orthography. Vanesa also added a musical symbol, a repeat sign, that asked the reader to say "Dad & Me" again—because once would not do for the level of intensity she wished to represent.

The heart might at first seem to be a straightforward, pictorial representation, but because it is meant not to represent an actual organ but rather the love in the relationship, it is more of a rebus, a word-like sign, and it is repeated in the upper-right and lower-left corners of the text. These corners are also inscribed in soft, comforting, curvilinear lines and other images of hope and renewal—stars, butterfly, flower. In the lower-right corner, with varying punctuation, are four commands to "sh!" which perhaps signify the comforting of a child, a "hush" like a lullaby, or parts of the story that will go unspoken. Either way, they sit in a borderzone between oral and literate modes of language. The restraint in these multimodal signs echoes the restraint in the written narrative, the large meanings that are assumed, unconfessed, and that have to be inferred to be understood, even as the piece overall seems effusive and expressive. The multimodal design of Vanesa's text, therefore, is another instance of hybridity, occupying a borderzone between pictorial and written media.

Vanesa's prose choices blended and crossed other linguistic and academic borders. Just like Nina, Vanesa employed spellings that are more conventional in texting such as "uu" and "ur" for "you" and "you're." And she assigned that form of social speech—which actually belonged to her and her peers—to her parents, making the reader wonder about her intention in doing so. Might it be, for instance, to portray the depth of love and closeness among her family that she would offer them a limited membership in a youth affinity group? The piece also blended genres. Written for a unit of study in "memoir," it avoids using conventional continuous prose, with dialogue written out as is common in novels or historical narratives. Though Vanesa is certainly familiar with narrative conventions for reporting speech from her own reading experience and her teacher's instruction, she shifted to a representation of orality that is more common in written play scripts or screenplays—the character name plus colon. By stepping out of a narrator's voice entirely, she left only the voices of the family members for the reader's attention, and so brought the reader closer into this intimate interaction.

This authorial decision yielded powerful results. For instance, her readers grasp that it is because her father is on the other side of a border that his call is so pivotal and capable of reviving Vanesa. The symbolic distance and absence that the border constructed in Vanesa's family life produced a longing in her that made her father's tenderness especially precious. Vanesa, as narrator, returned in a telling voice only to bring the reader inside her own thoughts, sitting there with her father on the phone: "His words make me stronger. He makes me feel alive!" Vanesa's memoir bore the theme of a transnational state of liminality, of in-betweenness (Bhabha, 1994), a borderzone consciousness deeply connected to the transnational realities of her private life, and she imported these transnational experiences along with her linguistic and multiliteracies repertoires to compose a compelling piece of academic writing for school.

Broader Forms of Critical Inquiry

Thus far, we have been taking a critical approach to the reading and writing curriculum, and learning how doing so can assist us in foregrounding transnationalism in literacy education. A transnationally aware curriculum would offer opportunities for students to undertake sustained critical study of their language and literacy practices and their lives, including the social, educational, economic, political, and other issues that concern them within and across local, national, and global communities. This dimension of our curriculum will frame our classrooms as learning spaces that are aware of, and responsive to, our students' lives in which they acquire important repertoires for learning. Broad forms of critical inquiry will provide avenues through which we can guide our students into exploring, questioning, and developing well-reasoned perspectives on culture, language, and literacy in social, academic, and other domains of life.

In Chapter 2, I discussed an approach to becoming transnationally literate that involved inquiring with our students into their language and literacy practices in and across multiple contexts. The inquiry project in which Molly and her students researched their literacy practices provided an example of this approach. We can create curricular space for one of these inquiry projects at the beginning of the school year. Also in Chapter 2, we touched on the idea of inquiring into our students' lived experiences within and across nations—with the examples of the self-portraiture, Coat of Arms, and Poster projects. We considered some questioning strategies that would begin guiding our students to think critically about their life experiences. We can plan for an initial critical inquiry project, and others across a school year, in which students investigate an issue that is of personal, familial, social, educational, or political significance to them on a local, national, or transnational scale, perhaps one they first signaled in a beginning-of-year assignment such as the self-portrait.

The timing and need for subsequent critical inquiry projects can materialize quite naturally in the classroom, as it did for Molly and her students who became seriously concerned about and invested in the situation in Haiti. As transnationally aware teachers, then, we would maintain a responsive stance to social justice concerns, both local and transnational, that arise for our students. But we can also strategically insert critical inquiry projects during ongoing curricular engagements across the school year. For example, just as Molly and her students returned to the stock of writing they had produced over several months of reading and writing to find a potential topic for extended composition, we can help our students identify the focus of an intentional inquiry by returning to earlier reading and writing, or to the body of knowledge we amassed (for instance, through the self-portraiture assignment) about their expansive identities and lived experiences. We can imagine, for example, transnational students like Vanesa and Nina wanting to investigate the transnational issue of human trafficking and sexual slavery that they learned about through reading the book *Sold*.

Whether we and our students return to earlier inquiry, reading, or writing; seize social and political opportunities that arise; or embark on critical inquiry without any clear reference to previous or immediate experience, we can conduct critical inquiry into the issues and contexts that matter to students in ways that help them generate critical knowledge, understandings, and stances as literate people in the world. I have engaged my own preservice teachers in a critical inquiry project in which we started cold—that is, with no specific issue as the topic of our research. Figure 3.4 is a copy of the assignment I created to take my teacher candidates on this journey, an assignment that, once they begin professional teaching, they often ask me to resend them so that they can conduct critical inquiries with their own middle and high school students.

Table 3.1 provides a review of the research methods and academic products we explored in Chapter 2 and also contains some additional ideas that will remain useful as we support our students in conducting a variety of critical inquiry projects throughout the school year.

Figure 3.4. Critical Inquiry Project Assignment

INQUIRY PROJECT GUIDELINES

Step One: Observation and Reflection

Week 1

Much of your work for this project will be assisted by the tool of a research journal. This assignment begins with you noticing and reflecting on the different contexts of your life to identify conditions or events that you have experienced, witnessed, or read/heard about that you feel are unfair, inequitable, or troubling. During this week, while you are out in schools and specific classrooms, or the larger community in which you or your students live, or while you're reading and watching the news, practice "reading" your surroundings with a heightened sense of awareness of social injustice. Begin keeping your journal this week. In it, describe and reflect on the issues of unfairness or injustice you are observing. You may keep your journal in a physical notebook, writing legibly in it, and dating each entry; type up your entries as separate dated documents and print them all out together at the end of the project; or create tagged entries on your class blog. You should write a minimum of four journal entries in this "observation and reflection" stage. Each entry should comprise a thoughtful reflection of about one page.

Please bring your research journal to class at the end of Week 1. On this date, your journal should contain a minimum of four entries. Each entry should be about one page in length.

Step Two: Identifying and Researching the Topic

Weeks 2 and 3

By the end of week 1, you must finalize your research topic choice. The next step is to conduct research into this issue. For example, if you are interested in an administrative practice or policy you have observed in a school that you think is unfair or that seems to have unfair consequences, you could begin by contacting the school district or searching its website for information on this policy to get the facts about it. You could also talk to students, teachers, and administrators about the policy to get their views about the intent of the policy, how it is being implemented at the school, and the ways in which the policy is and is not working well. If you are concerned about the in-school literacy performance of a particular student that you've been working with or observing, you should invite that student, her teacher(s), and possibly other people in her life to talk with you about her literacy history, in and out of school literate life, etc., perhaps toward gaining some insight about how school literacy work could be made more accessible for that student. If you are interested in the quality/prices/availability of healthy food in an underserved community in which your students live, you might begin by visiting some local stores to check out what's available, searching for government or local community groups that may already be looking into that problem and that can provide some insight into that issue, and talking with kids or families in that community to learn more about that issue from their perspective. As you conduct research, gather documents (policies, brochures, news articles, photographs, lists of websites, audio or video recordings or handwritten notes of conversations you have with key informants, etc.) that are helping you learn more about your topic.

(continued)

Figure 3.4. Critical Inquiry Project Assignment *(continued)*

You should be maintaining your research journal during these 2 weeks. In it, keep a record of the information you are finding and the places/people that you are collecting this data from. Additionally, write reflective notes on significant information you are finding and eye-opening conversations you are having with people, and just generally, your thoughts about what you are learning.

At the end of week 3, you must bring your research journal to class. Your journal should contain things like lists of the data you have so far, descriptions of places you have visited/ people you have contacted or spoken to about your topic, and reflective notes. Reflective notes contain your thinking about significant conversations you've had or noteworthy pieces of information you've found. At the end of week 3, you should also bring some documents that you have collected during the course of your research. You should continue documenting your research activities throughout the project, and you will turn in your research journal when the project concludes.

Completed Research Journal: 15 points

Step Three: Finalizing the Action Plan and Completing Your Report

Week 4

During this week, you should create an action plan and complete your research presentation. Your action plan involves taking stock of all you've learned from your inquiry, and from that knowledge base, thinking about what can be done or what more can be done toward improving the situation you've been studying. Your action plan could take the form of a written narrative or a bulleted list of well-developed and articulated ideas that speak to what an individual, group of persons, and/or organization could do to improve the condition you've been studying.

The final step of this project is to put together your research report. Your report will be an oral presentation accompanied by a research poster.

The research poster should include your research topic/research question, some examples of the data you collected, a summary (could be a few short, well-articulated sentences) of the most significant "findings"—things you learned from your research, and your action plan.

Plan to give a 10-minute oral presentation in which you will use your poster as a guide for addressing the major elements of your project. You should explain your topic and how you became interested in it; describe the process of data collection, highlighting important events that happened during that time or significant pieces of information you came across; and explain your action plan and why you think it will help improve the condition you studied. You could conclude by talking about how you are thinking about this project in relation to your work as an English or Social Studies literacy educator.

Oral Presentation: 5 points

Poster: 10 points

Table 3.1. Critical Inquiry Methods and Academic Products

Inquiry Methods	Academic Products
Finding, reading, and analyzing information from books and online sources including a variety of websites ranging from individual to institutional sites	Written or oral evaluations of the quality and credibility of websites (see Damico, Baildon, Exter, & Shiau-Jing, 2010, for an instructional model of how to teach students the skills of critically evaluating websites) Informational note-taking Annotated bibliographies Screen shots Written emails or phone calls to request additional information or clarification
Interviews and surveys	Create and administer interview protocols and surveys through physical and digital technologies Create charts, graphs, or written reports representing survey data
Self-studies of one's experiences with the topic of the critical inquiry	Autobiographical or memoir writing Write and stage a dramatic performance or video-record a short film highlighting the experience
Combined inquiry methods and data sources	A multimodal research report (e.g., combine audio- or video-recorded interviews, descriptive and numerical information, photographs and other artifacts)

A Generative Stance Toward Transnationalism in the Literacy Curriculum

The instructional approaches we explored across this chapter for connecting transnational and all other repertoires to the literacy curriculum function at their best when they are undergirded by our professional stance that our students' lives and repertoires are indispensable to teaching and learning. In closing this chapter, I offer a set of generative questions on which we, with our students, can continuously reflect and use to guide us in maintaining a generative stance toward transnationalism as we innovate our own unique curricular and instructional approaches that reflect such a stance.

- What academic literacies are we building together in this class?
- What are our other goals for growing as literate people?
- How might transnationalism as a concept and a way of life fit with our goals for learning the official curriculum?

- How might our transnational knowledge, experiences, languages, and literacies assist our purposes and processes for learning the official curriculum?
- How might transnationalism as a concept and way of life help us notice additional purposes and processes for engaging with literacy in this class?
- How might our transnational knowledge, experiences, languages, and literacies help us identify new objectives for literacy learning in this class?

We can display and revisit these questions across units of study to continuously orient our students and ourselves toward recruiting and strengthening our students' transnational knowledge, languages, and literacies in literacy learning as we also draw upon and bolster the other resources for teaching and learning that all our students bring to school. In the next chapter, we will extend our professional learning regarding how transnationalism can further inform teaching and learning in our classrooms by exploring the ways in which our educational practices can support our transnational students' literacy education in the other nations in which they go to school.

CHAPTER 4

Learning for Teaching Across Transnational School Settings

Beginning with Chapter 1, we noted a defining feature of life for some transnational youths—receiving formal education in one or more schools in different countries. I connected this phenomenon to the interstate or intraregional movements that mononational students can undertake that result in their leaving our classrooms or schools for a time and sometimes returning. Transnationalism greatly emphasizes the phenomenon of formal learning that is stretched across school settings because transnational lifestyles introduce greater diversity in the cultural, linguistic, economic, and educational conditions in which our students learn. Beginning with the self-portraiture and other assignments in Chapter 2, we began to learn about the transnational and local settings in which our students experience school. We have thus been preparing ourselves to engage with the primary goal of this chapter: to help us develop ways to support our transnational students' academic development in classrooms other than our own—classrooms that may be located in different countries or different regions of our own country. What we learn about supporting our transnational students' learning in other contexts will apply to our efforts to remain involved in and supportive of any of our students who will be leaving our classroom community, whether or not they plan to return. Therefore, although we will be exploring the ideas in this chapter directly through the lens of transnationalism, we will make many natural connections to the work of supporting the academic development of any and all of our students who may receive parts of their literacy education in other classrooms.

The chapter first identifies some key knowledge and understandings that teachers of transnational youths need to acquire about the different formal school settings to which our students are connected. It suggests how we, along with our students, can learn about pertinent transnational schools and what different educational conditions can mean for transnational students' academic development. The chapter then explores the unique demands of transnational education that require creating shared knowledge and conditions for teaching and learning across transnational schools and transitioning transnational students across those settings. It provides some strategies we can use to collaborate with other teachers, students, families, and various stakeholders to plan for, execute, and support those transitions. Finally, the chapter discusses some curricular and instructional approaches that teachers of transnational youths can use to stay abreast of and to participate in our students' formal education across transnational contexts or across different schools students may attend within one country. Monica, a transnational youth with origins in St. Maarten, will demonstrate the sharp educational ruptures that students can experience, thus impressing on us the need to provide academic support to our transnational students who must navigate education across transnational life.

RUNNING WHILE GOING BACKWARDS: MONICA'S EXPERIENCE OF TRANSNATIONAL EDUCATIONAL RUPTURES

Monica was born in Dutch St. Maarten. Her mother, Cherise, immigrated to the island from Curaçao, another Dutch-speaking Caribbean island, where she met Monica's father, a native citizen of St. Maarten. Monica's father lived a transnational lifestyle for economic purposes; he had worked on St. Maarten as well as in Connecticut and Florida in the United States. Monica had lived with her mother in St. Maarten as a young child and her early schooling occurred there in a Dutch language school. Since she was 9, however, Monica had lived and gone to school in central Florida, where her father and stepmother lived, but she spent summers and other holidays with her mother in St. Maarten. During the middle of her junior year of high school in Florida, Monica's father decided to take a new job opportunity in St. Maarten, a decision that was also partly influenced by he and his wife's divorce. Monica was thus suddenly returned to St. Maarten and reinstated in school there, a decision in which she had little input and about which she was quite upset. As Monica described it,

> My dad divorced my stepmom, and he was unemployed, so we just moved down here [to St. Maarten] because they had better jobs. When he told me [we were moving to St. Maarten] I was pretty mad because I was going in my last year [of high school]. . . . It wasn't really something I could say about it. It was "We are going." So . . . I couldn't say, my judgment wasn't really anything. Because he had a better job here and he had everything signed. It was pretty much, "Yeah, we are going to St. Maarten."

From the onset, re-enrolling in school in St. Maarten caused grave difficulties for Monica. One major problem was the national curriculum language requirement that all students take and pass 3 years of Dutch in order to receive a high school diploma. Monica had long since lost her fluency in Dutch, so this requirement led school personnel to place her in the equivalent of 9th grade (rather than in her final year of secondary school), to ensure that she would have time to relearn the language and meet the language requirement. Being placed several grades behind her academic abilities created yet another set of educational problems for Monica—disengagement and a lack of challenge.

> They pushed me back 2 years, so 'cause of the Dutch system, they do not want me to struggle through it and fail the Dutch. But they are saying I am too advanced for third form, but then they don't want to push me up 'cause of Dutch. So it's kind of like back and forth. The Dutch classes are really hard for me because they are on like, they [students] are reading Dutch. Like they've read it for years now, and I am just reading it. So, it is like I should be walking in baby steps, instead I am running. Other classes are easy. English is really, really, really easy. But they are teaching us how to put sentences together still and put words or definitions of words that should have already been known, but so it's like . . . I'm going backwards.

WHAT IS THERE TO LEARN ABOUT TRANSNATIONAL SCHOOL SETTINGS?

The transnational educational experiences of youths are as distinctive as the international contexts to which they have ties and their unique lived experiences of transnationalism. Transnational students like Monica sometimes undergo formal schooling for extended periods of time in different nations. Other transnational youths cross borders more frequently and so attend school in different countries (and even different schools in particular countries) across 1 or more academic years. For other students, transnational border crossings result in interrupted formal schooling, an issue I will address in the following chapter. When our students undertake formal schooling in another nation as part of their transnational lifestyle, we need to have a broad understanding of how education works in the nation(s) in which our students go to school. I use the phrase "educational policies and schooling structures" to describe that general educational landscape of nations' schooling systems. As teachers, we also need to know about the common curricular and instructional approaches used in the particular regions or schools to which our transnational students are most directly connected. I will discuss each of these two broad domains below and show why and how this knowledge is beneficial for us as teachers of transnational youths, and more generally, for supporting our mononational students when they head off to other schools and literacy classrooms.

Educational Policies and Schooling Structures

For our transnational students, it is important that we gain a sense of the educational options that are available to them across transnational life. For example, we need to know whether the other nations in which our students attend school subsidize the entirety of its children's education or whether families must pay for some or all of students' schooling, which is the case in some countries. This kind of information will help us understand why schools in particular countries have or lack certain resources, and why our students have or do not have access to particular educational options or experiences in a certain country. Learning about educational conditions in other places will make us more aware and understanding of the kinds of formal academic experiences and growth that are possible for our students while they are in a particular country. This knowledge will also be useful to our understanding of the educational opportunities available for any of our students—whether they are transnational or mononational—who will be leaving our classrooms to attend school in another region of our country.

As one example, in terms of transnational educational access, some Caribbean nations operate according to a system of general and high-stakes examinations that slot students into different secondary schools with differing academic emphases, rigor, and outcomes. This system is often described as the "British system." If, in the middle of a school year, a transnational student leaves a country like the United States that does not organize schooling in this way and enters a Caribbean context with such policies, that student will likely be placed (barring social contacts and advocacy) in a school of lower status because he or she will not have taken the national entrance examination. Monica experienced the effects of these kinds of national educational policies. The school she attended when she returned to St. Maarten was an English-run school that served students who had done poorly on the national exams or who were immigrants, transnational youths, or otherwise newcomers to St. Maarten's schools. This school had a reputation for high teacher and student absenteeism and low academic expectations for students. Monica described a frequently occurring situation:

> Sometimes you walk in to the school and the teacher is not there. There's no class. . . . In the States, if there wasn't a teacher there was a substitute so we are still learning from someone else teaching us, but yeah, there's a lot of times I come to school and I come to school for nothing because there is no class. . . . And most teachers, they just . . . give us an assignment and when we get it done, we leave. So, sometimes I am in the classroom not even 20 minutes because I know this already, so I just do it and then I leave. . . . We have benches out in the front [of the school] and we just sit or just hang out or something.

Monica told me she had been placed in this school as a "mostly temporary" solution because another school she was eligible to attend was full at the time. Even so, given the academically tiered structure of schooling, Monica knew that "the new school I will go to, it's a little bit lower than other schools. So, I don't really know if [the new school] is different [meaning, better] teaching" [from her current school]. This new school to which Monica hoped to transfer was run according to a different set of educational policies and structures. It followed what Sasha, another transnational youth who received her K–12 schooling in St. Maarten, described to me as English-run schools that aligned with the "U.S.-based" educational system. United States–based schools in St. Maarten, Sasha said, have "the same education system as the U.S. schools. Like they do the whole GPA, all of that . . . A, B, same grading system . . . they do the SAT . . . the curriculum is structured like the United States." Parents often thought about international higher education options when choosing secondary schools. The United States–based secondary school structure in St. Maarten lent itself well to students who wanted to matriculate into U.S. colleges and universities. As Sasha understood it, "I guess it's like maybe easier for you to just follow through and go to college in the United States if you already did the U.S. curriculum."

Beyond the structure of schools, language can be an overriding factor as families make decisions about where their children will attend school across transnational life. And language can heavily shape the academic resources that students are permitted to access as well as their academic success. Monica's experience with the Dutch language in education illustrates this phenomenon. Countries that have a colonial past, such as Dutch St. Maarten, sometimes offer high-quality, free public schools where the language of instruction is that of the colonizer. As Sasha explained to me, the only students who typically completed their education in those schools were those whose parents are Dutch. Sasha herself was educated in a Dutch language-run school until 2nd grade at which time her parents, who are Dominican immigrants to St. Maarten and native English speakers, switched her to a public English-run school. This was a common decision for families like Sasha's, she explained: "Here in my country [St. Maarten] it is common that your parents will not actually be from St. Maarten, so their first language most likely won't be Dutch. So it is harder for them to help you in school if they can't speak the language you are learning in."

Getting into a high-quality "British" or "U.S."-based, English-run school was a competitive affair, given the high number of English-speaking families living on St. Maarten. St. Maarten, historically and currently, holds the number-one spot of receiving countries in intra-Caribbean migration (Cepal.org, 2002; Government of Sint Maarten, 2014). Transnational children like Monica who were latecomers in the school year would not have opportunities to secure a spot in a high-quality English-run school like the one Sasha attended. Being newcomers who also do not speak the language of the colonizer, these students have restricted choices among the English-run schools that have open seats, but which are often of lower quality. And, as we have seen from Monica's case, schools that are run in a language that transnational students know still retain the national language study requirement, that of the colonizer, which causes academic difficulties for the youths. Finally, families' social class and economic conditions compound the issue of schooling options for transnational students. For instance, as Monica and her mother ruminated with me about the educational options available to Monica on St. Maarten, her mother shared that there were private, English-run schools on the island that were not beholden to the country's Dutch language requirement. Monica's mother, however, a saleswoman in a jewelry store who had also just given birth to a baby boy, could not afford the $9,000 annual tuition she reported such schools would charge to educate her daughter.

Educational options for youths across transnational life are thus arranged differently, and families' decisionmaking about schooling involves complex analyses that involve social class, culture, language, and academic opportunity. These factors are similar to those mononational families consider when they are moving intranationally or intraregionally. However, for transnational as well as mononational families, these educational arrangements are more complex than a benign set of educational options or educational structures. They must be viewed from critical perspectives that identify and critique the historical, sociopolitical, sociolinguistic, socioeconomic, and sociocultural factors that combine to manufacture such schooling options that create or foreclose opportunity for students and families based on their social class, life experiences, and national and linguistic affiliations. As teachers who aim to gain knowledge about the educational settings to which our transnational and other students have ties, we must analyze that knowledge through such critical lenses. We can use what we learn to assist and advocate for students and families who are deciding on formal schooling options that will work best for them, a topic I take up later in this chapter.

Curriculum and Pedagogical Approaches

Beyond understanding the organization of schools in other countries or regions in which our transnational or mononational students attend school, we will also benefit from knowing about the curriculum and pedagogical approaches used in those schools. Such knowledge will provide us with a reasonable sense of how our own curriculum and pedagogy can prepare all of our students—regardless of transnational status—for success in different school contexts, how we can support our students academically while they are away, and how we will need to meet them where they are if and when they return to our classrooms. Ideological understandings of what curriculum, teaching, and learning should look like can be quite different, particularly across national contexts, but also, as we know, across schools and communities within one region or nation. For instance, some Caribbean schools still practice forms of teaching and learning that, in the United States and Canada, would be considered rote approaches. Students, teachers, and families in the Caribbean often value these traditional forms of teaching, with students often achieving at high academic levels and reporting engagement with the curriculum and pedagogy in their classrooms. This is not to say that all teachers in the Caribbean teach with those methods or that such instructional approaches work for all students throughout the Caribbean. Sometimes, for the transnational students who flourish under those pedagogies, it is only after being exposed to different instructional approaches in other nations that they notice and critique the differences.

For instance, Monica was able to identify clear differences in curriculum and pedagogical styles between her secondary English classes in Florida and St. Maarten.

> I remember in the States we did essays, reading Shakespeare, to reading a whole bunch of different books and we'll talk about it. It was more

> on written [novels] or on biography and stuff like that. And here [in St. Maarten] it's just you go into class, you read a story, you answer passages, and you have definitions for words, and you figure what's wrong with punctuation sentences. That's what they mostly do here. I can't recall . . . I've been here since June and I can't recall having read one book. Like, they don't give us books to read. It is just a workbook. . . . I don't know. . . . I like it here. I just wish the schools were the same.

Sasha, too, described differences in English language arts curriculum and pedagogy across her upper secondary classes in St. Maarten and her first semester at a suburban/rural campus of a New York state college.

> My English teacher [in St. Maarten], who was from Jamaica, spoke with a British accent [laughs]. She was very strict. The things we did in class, it was a lot of reading, like just reading, reading, [and] we did very technical aspect of writing. They [St. Maarten schools] focus a lot, which I think all schools do, on like grammar and spelling, punctuation. All these things, it's like very reserved, very important to them. To the point like you can get a five-point deduction for this. Even if your writing is good, but if your, your grammar is off a little bit, you can get major deductions for just that. Every student was kind of taught the same. There wasn't really an individuality type thing. . . . So, that's how it was in high school in terms of the teacher. . . .
>
> With my English course in [an upstate New York] college now, which surprised me because I expected to be something similar, it was completely opposite. They [instructors] are very into individualism, so they won't even grade you on a specific scale. Like, every student is graded differently based on their abilities, their style of writing. We did study writing, just like in high school with Shakespeare, etc. But the way we did it [in New York], it was like, it was from a very artistic standpoint versus the technical standpoint. Like, even if your writing had spelling errors or grammatic [*sic*] errors or like flawed context or layout, you can still get an A. Not because they are giving you an easy grade, but because they are focusing on what you were trying to say versus how you said it. And then they would personally help you with what you, how to say it in a better way. . . . And they would show us writing of the Greats [classic authors], but like the original writing, not the finished product. The writing where they are scratching out, and they are like, "This looks just like your papers when you are working."

From their transnational experiences of English education, Monica and Sasha developed sophisticated understandings and critiques of different approaches to the teaching and learning of literacy and were able to identify which aspects of literacy curriculum and instruction best supported their own engagement and learning.

These students' transnational understandings about literacy education were not just confined to English education, and their analyses did not always favor U.S.

educational practices. For as long as she could remember, Sasha always elected to take music classes in school in Dutch St. Maarten. Sasha also explored music as a minor in her U.S. college but grew disappointed with what she felt was the overly theoretical focus of the music education program. She couched her comparison of music education in St. Maarten and the United States as a "comparison [that] would be kind of opposite" to her comparison of English education across those two countries.

> I remember music class in high school [in St. Maarten], which I preferred that class over the one I did in New York. I don't know if it is because of the culture or the specific area in the United States I am studying, but there [her New York college], the music program is very technical. It is very straightforward theory. Lots of focus on classical . . . it is very focused on the technical aspect, the reading, the writing, the literal format of composition, etc., etc. I mean within the whole time I did the music class, I don't really remember playing, hearing. Like maybe a few times around the whole semester, but barely literally hearing music. Just this one time we sat and listened or did an activity that actually pertained to doing music. Whereas here [in St. Maarten], in music, in high school, we did get theory, but they focused a lot more on the actual playing, listening, observing of different types of music. Even if you didn't sing too well or play too well, you still get a, you would still be acknowledged or like praised for expressing yourself artistically. So I guess here [in St. Maarten], in terms of music, I preferred it, the way it was done. Because it was more about the music itself versus being technical. It was about the soul of the music versus the format.

As Sasha talked more about these transnational differences in music education, she teased out ideas about culture, geographic region, and the ideological and structural elements of school and society that likely contributed to those differences. Sasha acknowledged how a U.S. school that was "an art school itself" might be "more expressive," and mentioned that she and a friend had discussed how race, culture, and region might affect particular approaches to music education. "I don't know, if maybe I studied music in the city [New York City] or lower down in the south [the southern United States]" it would be different rather than the "more suburban type place, predominantly White" space that was her upstate New York college. As a consequence of transnational education that exposed her to different curricula and pedagogies, Sasha was able to notice different ways of teaching, learning, and engaging in music across transnational educational settings. The different physical transnational settings of music, and the distinctive beliefs, norms, and practices of being "musical" that governed each space, enabled Sasha to experience different structures, processes, and practices of being a musician.

Sasha's and Monica's stories illustrate that sociocultural traditions and ideological beliefs about effective educational practice result in students and teachers in particular settings valuing certain educational approaches even though those same practices are not greatly valued in other educational contexts. Understanding our transnational students' educational experiences in other lands will give us insights into how a transnational youth may be experiencing curriculum, teaching, and learning in our classrooms in light of other educational experiences or beliefs the student has encountered. In the same vein, knowing how all of our students have experienced literacy curriculum and instruction in other classrooms will help us better understand their social and academic responses to our approaches to literacy education.

INSTRUCTIONAL APPROACHES FOR LEARNING ABOUT TRANSNATIONAL SCHOOL SETTINGS

In my role as a researcher, I gained deep knowledge about and insights into youths' educational options and academic experiences across transnational life by inviting them to share their stories of transnational education with me. I also sought out additional information from informants who were knowledgeable about the youths' transnational lives and education in the contexts in which they lived. Finally, I conducted independent research about education in the countries in which the youths lived and attended school. As teachers, we can use similar methods with our students to learn about the transnational (or other intranational) schooling contexts that are relevant to their educational lives. In this section, I elaborate on some strategies for gaining such knowledge.

Inquiries into Relevant Transnational School Settings

We have already explored the idea of inquiry into our transnational and mononational students' prior schooling experiences beginning with the self-portraiture assignment in Chapter 2 and the in-depth discussion in Chapter 3 about inquiry as a curricular approach for connecting transnationalism to the literacy curriculum. If our transnational students have undertaken an inquiry project into schooling as part of our general literacy curriculum, we will already have become familiar with some of the details of their transnational schooling experiences. I suggested some key dimensions of schooling for students conducting such an inquiry to research about:

- different options for schooling;
- language(s) of instruction;
- cultural demographics and descriptions;
- curricular texts, topics, and emphases across grade levels;
- instructional approaches teachers use and students enjoy; and
- common learning activities and assessments.

We also worked our way through a number of research activities such as gathering data from online sources and conducting interviews, and academic products such as multimodal research reports or case studies that students could engage with and generate from this work. As particular students prepare to depart from one country to another transnational location (or to a different geographic region within the same country in which we teach), it will be helpful for us to sit with them and review any relevant research they have already conducted on schooling in that country or region as a way to begin preparing for the transition, an issue I will take up shortly in further detail. This kind of information will help us understand our transnational students' educational experiences and opportunities.

If our students have not undertaken such an inquiry, and particularly if they are about to leave our classroom to enter school in another country, we can conduct our own investigation about schooling in the country our students are about to enter using these same research methods. We can invite the transnational student to assist us as a research partner, and perhaps even seek the help of a family member or other informant who is involved in the life and education of that student. Seeking help may become especially important if language and cultural issues arise as we do this kind of research. Our transnational students, families, and community members can serve as cultural insiders and linguistic brokers for us by helping us make sense of written texts and also to understand the social, cultural, historical, and political landscape that influences how education functions in that context.

Building Transnational Relationships with Educational Partners

As we learn with our students about their schooling contexts, we will identify key educational stakeholders in other transnational or local settings with whom we need to build relationships. For instance, we or one of our students might learn from doing research that the curriculum emphasis in our literacy class is similar to that of a particular grade level of a school in a TC 2 or TC 1 context that the student will attend at some point. Sasha's explanation about the curricular similarities between some St. Maarten and U.S. schools suggests it is possible that transnational students or their teachers will discover such a connection. If we notice these connections, we can try to establish contact and build a relationship with one or two teachers in that grade level or in the language arts department at this school in another context. Some students currently in our care may already have supportive relationships with teachers and peers in a school they have previously attended, and they and their families may be able to introduce us to those teachers and classrooms.

Our transnational students and families will also understand how teachers are viewed and positioned culturally in that other society and its schools, which can give us some insight into how we, their colleagues from another country, can approach them with an awareness of their cultural and professional norms. As we have seen in the research on transnational and, more generally, culturally and linguistically diverse youths, our students possess an impressive repertoire of linguistic and cultural skills, including sophisticated capacities in cultural and linguistic brokering among themselves and adults (Orellana & Reynolds, 2008). Thus, teachers of transnational and other diverse youths likely have untapped linguistic and cultural resources in our classrooms that can help us learn about transnational and other educational settings that may differ from our own in terms of language and culture.

Just as we used digital literacies to research the inter- and intranational educational settings in which our students have gone to school, we can establish and maintain transnational educational relationships through digital literacies such as email, Facebook, or other digital communications if they are available across pertinent settings. Traditional mail can work well too, if that is all that's available. Nina, one of the transnational youths whose memoir you read in the previous chapter, recalled how in 3rd grade her teacher connected the students in her class with children in another country as pen pals: "I had a pen pal in 3rd grade and they were in 5th grade . . . they were like from another country. . . . And we would write to each other and we would send pictures too. I thought it was pretty cool." As with building any kind of professional partnerships, we should certainly expect challenges. The work of building transnational educational relationships may indeed be even more complicated because it involves establishing relationships across nations, cultures, and sometimes language differences among professionals, families, and youths who are already busy each day. Nonetheless, we can think of any of our efforts toward building transnational educational relationships as a significant counterpoint to the current problematic situation, where transnational students and their families lack any professional support as they undertake their journeys into other schooling contexts. These relationships can serve as another way, beyond the research we undertake with our students, to acquire some of the knowledge we need about transnational educational settings, such as educational options and curricular and instructional emphases.

APPROACHES FOR TRANSITIONING AND TEACHING ACROSS TRANSNATIONAL SCHOOL SETTINGS

Transnational youths and their teachers experience the unique challenge of educational disruption caused by the youths' frequent border crossings or extended residencies in different nations (Hamann & Zúñiga, 2011). Along with our students, we can use the knowledge we acquire about transnational educational settings to ease the sharp ruptures caused by transnational education. Moreover, we can use this knowledge to devise strategies for supporting our transnational students' literacy education across national borders. Below, I will explore some approaches and activities we can use, with our students and their families, to plan for and accomplish smoother transitions in and out of transnational school settings. I will also describe some strategies we can use to stay aware and supportive of, as well as involved in, our transnational students' learning in other educational contexts. All the ideas we will explore—participating in decisions about schooling, writing letters of support, sharing our curriculum with other teachers, and writing individualized academic plans for students—have direct relevance for providing professional and academic support to any and all of our students who are transitioning from our classroom into other educational settings, including those within one country.

Participating in Decisions About Schooling Options

We can play key roles as consultants and advocates who work with our transnational students and their families to secure appropriate transnational schooling placements for students. If we and our students have conducted inquiries into their previous educational experiences, including those involving transnational education, we will have some knowledge about the educational context into which our transnational students are going. Understanding the potential educational options for a particular student may be a part of this transnational educational knowledge. We should remember, however, from our earlier discussion, that decisions about schooling are complex affairs that include cultural, economic, and other factors—thus, families' decisions about schooling for their children can be a very private affair—one for which we, as teachers, need to show the utmost respect. That being said, students and families, particularly those who have come to know that we are teachers who are invested in and knowledgeable about their children's transnational circumstances, and who are seeking advice, may ask our opinions as they make decisions about schooling in another country. Even if our students and their families do not ask our advice, we can show them that we have cared enough to learn about the educational landscape in another country they call home, and we may choose to tell them that we are happy to participate in those conversations if they wish us to.

Vanesa's mother solicited my advice about schooling options for Vanesa as the family planned for an extended return to Mexico, asking my opinions about what kinds of curricular elements she should keep in mind when selecting a new high school for Vanesa in Mexico, particularly because the family wished for Vanesa to attend college in the United States. The family had already determined that Vanesa would need to maintain and further develop her social and academic competency in English. Vanesa was also advocating strongly for continuing her instruction in dance, which she had taken as a curricular elective at Southwest High School. The family asked me what I knew about the entrance requirements at the university where I taught and what characteristics I thought they should look for in a college or university for Vanesa, given my knowledge of her social and academic strengths and needs. Furthermore, we discussed Vanesa's options or opportunities for qualifying for financial aid and various scholarships to attend college in the United States if she completed the remaining years of her secondary education in Mexico, as opposed to if she continued her education transnationally, across both countries. In my role as a caring professional involved in Vanesa's life, the family saw me as an important source of information, although they maintained control over their own decisionmaking process.

As we do research into transnational educational contexts, we and our students may identify or establish relationships with a teacher or school in the country our student is heading to. If this happens, we can rely on those relationships as we plan with the student and family for the transition. For instance, we can ask advice from a transnational teacher colleague about an appropriate school placement for the youth if the student and family wish us to do so. Alternatively, we might ask the teacher to suggest people or strategies that we and the family can pursue to obtain the information needed. Of course, transnational students and their families will also have other family members, friends, and/or social groups such as religious organizations in the transnational location to which they are headed. They will certainly ask about schooling options within their own social networks. Family members, close friends, or other concerned stakeholders within social or institutional organizations can help locate particular kinds of information that the family needs about certain schools. Those stakeholders can also serve as proxies or advocates for transnational students and their families in conversations with people at those schools.

Writing Letters of Support and Advocacy

In the same way that we advocate for our students within the schools and communities where we teach, we can provide explicit kinds of advocacy that reach into another country. One way teachers can advocate for a transnational student to secure an appropriate school placement is by writing a letter describing the student's academic strengths, accomplishments, and learning needs. We, or the student's family, can transmit this letter digitally (or physically) to administrators or teachers in the receiving transnational school. We can also suggest that the family ask other teachers, guidance counselors, or a principal in our school for a similar letter of support. Or we can simply circulate the letter we write to the student's other teachers and our principal, asking them for signatures of support. This strategy is just as useful for providing educational support and advocacy for students who are leaving for literacy classrooms in the next grade level of our school, in neighboring schools, or more distant regions within our country as it is for transnational students.

Sharing Curriculum Plans Across Transnational School Settings

We are used to discussing our curriculum and teaching, and the academic development of the students in our care, with relevant educational partners. We can broaden these practices transnationally by serving as curriculum informants and brokers who share our general curriculum plans and academic plans for providing specific learning supports for the transnational students we share with the appropriate transnational teachers. We would count ourselves quite fortunate if, at the transition stages, we discover that our transnational students will be entering literacy classrooms or schools with which we have previous relationships—for instance, from conducting previous inquiry with our students into their transnational educational experiences. It may, however, be more typical for us to find out to which specific school or literacy classroom one of our transnational students is headed near the point of the actual transition. Still, we may have an opportunity to establish some cross-national professional dialogue about curriculum and instruction so we and our transnational teacher colleagues can give and receive a useful picture of what teaching and learning looks like in our classrooms. We can share curricular information with a teacher in another country via a link to a class website or Facebook page—digital presences that some of us already use to share our classroom with others. We could also share curriculum information through an email exchange. Where digital technologies are not available, we can use physical transportation—for example, entrusting documents to the care of our transnational students and their families as they cross over into other transnational homes and literacy classrooms.

Below is a list of items that teachers can provide their colleagues, be they transnational teachers or other educational partners, which will paint a picture of teaching and learning in our classrooms:

- The broad curriculum plan for the year
- Instructional processes and accompanying materials we are engaging—for example, inquiry and text genres
- Major learning projects we are taking on
- Educational objectives and learning goals we are pursuing across a school year

We can compile this information easily, drawing from the following:

- Our yearly curriculum plan, which might be in a calendar format or a chronological list of the units of study including teaching and learning objectives and activities and major assessments
- More detailed syllabi or unit plans that we originally created for ourselves or to share with our students, their families, or colleagues within our school
- The official literacy curriculum documents or standards of our department, school, or school district
- Another format or combination of documents that works for us and that would involve just drawing from existing documents we have already created or that we utilize in the normal course of planning for teaching

We would want to frame our sharing of curricular information in ways that establish and emphasize mutual professional regard and interest between our transnational teacher colleagues and us. Our goal is to provide information that the teachers receiving our students might find useful in understanding the students' previous academic knowledge and experiences and that can give them some immediate insights into how their own teaching and curriculum would relate to the students as learners. To further build mutual professional respect, we would also encourage the teacher(s) with whom we have shared those curriculum documents (or, after they arrive, the student and family) to share with us information about the literacy curriculum in that context. Similar to what we share with our transnational students' teachers, the information the teachers share can take the form of official curriculum standards documents available at the school, the teacher's course syllabi, or a simple outline of a year's academic plan. In all of this, we would want to depend on our transnational students, their families, or other cultural insiders to be sure that we are inviting relationship, dialogue, and curricular sharing within acceptable cultural and professional norms in the pertinent transnational context.

Having curriculum documents from another country in hand allows us to analyze and consider how literacy education across two national contexts complement and diverge from each other. These analyses afford us and our transnational teacher colleagues mutual understandings of the curriculum and instructional emphases in each context with which our shared students must engage. This kind of sharing and analysis will help all of us teach, and our transnational students learn, with greater awareness of the demands of literacy education across the two countries. Thinking back to Monica's case, we can imagine that her teachers in St. Maarten would be interested in the kinds of literacy pedagogy Monica experienced and valued in her U.S. school. Having some tangible curriculum documents that suggested how Monica's literacy teachers in Florida enacted that pedagogy might stir her St. Maarten teachers' thinking about the potential and limitations of these curricula and pedagogies for Monica, for other students, and for their teaching within their particular schooling context.

Monica's teachers in Florida would also benefit from learning about and analyzing Monica's literacy education in St. Maarten. Similar to Vanesa and her family's ongoing processing of Vanesa's schooling options, as Monica attended school in St. Maarten, she, her mother, and family friends in both St. Maarten and Florida were actively considering whether Monica should return to Florida to complete high school. In one conversation I listened in on, a family friend whose sister lived in southwest Florida reminded Monica and her mother, "Remember [my sister] said she would take Monica?" I noticed Monica's hesitation as she responded, "Yes. But it would be living again with someone I don't know. And my mom doesn't have anyone and I have to help [her] with the baby. . . . I'll think about it." Monica's deliberations illustrated the impermanency and flux of transnational living arrangements. There was a strong possibility that Monica would reappear in the U.S. classrooms that she had left. Thus, if Monica's U.S. teachers stayed informed about her academic experiences in St. Maarten, that knowledge could help them reintegrate Monica into those learning communities if she did return. Knowledge of curricular contexts equips each transnational teacher with a good sense of who our students are at the particular points in time that they come to us and helps us identify the kinds of academic support we need to offer them as they cross and recross national educational borders.

Sharing information about curriculum, teaching, and learning in our classrooms is something all of us already do as teachers. Many of us already prepare curriculum documents to share with our students, their families, or the new teachers who will be receiving our students in the upper grades or teaching courses in which we are experts. When we share information with families, we often take into consideration language and cultural differences. To communicate across these differences, we already ask our students who know the target language for help with translating documents, or we ask others in our school or community who know the language for assistance. There are also websites that can sometimes assist with translation such as Google Translate (https://translate.google.com/). However, any tools like these will need to be used with a critical and human eye that is sensitive to changes in social, cultural, and literal meanings that can occur in the process of translation. For this reason, it would remain important to work with transnational students or other community members who have some knowledge of the languages and cultures of interest when we translate documents.

It becomes more critical for teachers to share with and learn from one another about curriculum and instruction and other aspects of education when transnational youths are involved because these youths' education is stretched across countries. As teachers of transnational youths, we need a good understanding of what is happening in all the schools and classrooms in which our students are being educated. This knowledge will help us envision the academic learning possibilities for our students in other countries. It will also help us support our students as they transition in and out of different transnational schools and learn successfully across them.

Creating an Individualized Academic Plan for the Transnational Student

One very specific way we can provide academic support for transnational students (or any of our students who will be leaving for other schools) is to create a concrete academic plan, uniquely designed to support a particular student's learning. The academic plan should take a strength- and asset-based view of students. One way this perspective can come across in our writing of the academic plan is to introduce that document by describing the academic strengths students already possess that will support their success in their new learning context. Speaking of our transnational students, our knowledge of students as learners and knowledge about the curriculum in the receiving transnational educational context will help us position students in an appreciative light that demonstrates their capacities for academic success in their new school. This transnational curricular knowledge and our knowledge of students as learners will also help us identify the information and skills our students will need to learn in the schools to which they are headed, the challenges that may arise in those learning environments, and possible ways to support students in meeting those challenges. Let's imagine that Monica had been our student. The introduction of the academic plan we create for Monica might go something like this:

> Monica is a smart, friendly, young woman who enjoys our English language arts class. Our class runs according to what is called a "workshop" approach (Bomer, 2011). Students choose the books they would like to read, read independently during class and at home, and talk with me, their teacher, and with their classmates about their reading. Sometimes we use book clubs where small groups of students choose a book they want to read and talk about it with one another for 2 or 3 weeks at a time. At certain points, we come together as a class to read and discuss a shared text. Our reading is accompanied by lots of writing. Students write what they are thinking about the books they are reading in what we call a reader's notebook. We also explore strategies for helping students understand, enjoy, and discuss the books they are reading. I teach these strategies in short lessons and give students opportunities to try out these strategies as they read their books.
>
> We also do longer learning units on writing. When we read a whole text together, students write a literary analysis essay, and I teach short lessons to help students craft that specific kind of essay. For other longer writing units, we choose specific genres, such as poetry, and read and study how texts in a particular genre are put together. Students then go through a lengthy process of writing, revising, and publishing their work—for example, reading their pieces at special school events that their families and friends attend.
>
> Monica is very strong in her abilities to enjoy, read, write, and talk about a wide range of texts in small- and whole-group discussion formats. She can write in a range of genres and for multiple purposes. She can write literary analyses of complex works of literature and informal responses to literature in a reader's notebook. She knows how to use a writer's notebook to brainstorm ideas for writing, to draft outlines for long pieces of work, and to use those outlines to write, revise, and complete pieces of work that are interesting, creative, and polished in terms of grammar, mechanics, and form. Monica has a wide vocabulary and typically learns new words in the context of her reading and through talking about texts with others. The "workshop" approach that Monica has experienced in our class has taught her how to read, write, and think independently and with others, and develop her oral and written language skills. She is excited to join your classroom and continue developing academically.

In what I wrote above, I tried to show how we can focus our task on providing a very clear description to our fellow teachers about what teaching and learning has looked like for the transnational student we share. If, from our analysis of curriculum across transnational settings, we conclude that our curriculum and learning objectives are similar to those in the transnational schools that our students will be attending, we will feel confident that our students will continue to strengthen the academic capacities they have been building in our classroom. Even if, as is the case for Monica, we realize there are distinct differences in instructional approaches or learning emphases across schools in two countries, we want to avoid giving the impression that our ideologies and curricular and instructional practices are "better" or more useful for the student. We would remind ourselves that there are different cultural, historical, ideological, and other factors that shape the nature of literacy education in different national contexts (and even different English classrooms in one school!). Thus, our genuine goal in the introductory section of the academic plan should be to inform our transnational colleagues about what literacy education has been like for the student of interest and how the student has responded socially and academically to our particular approach to literacy education. These other teachers will conduct their own analysis of our approach to teaching and learning (as we have done of theirs) and arrive at their own conclusions about whether and in what ways the information we have shared will inform their own practice in general and with the particular student.

In introducing this chapter, I noted that there are diverse configurations of transnational educational life. Some transnational students may leave our classroom, enroll in a school in another country (or in a school in some other region of our country), and return to our classroom within the space of months. Other transnational students may leave our classrooms for another country during or at the end of an academic year with no firm plan to return either to our school or to the country in which we teach them. This diversity of educational arrangements applies even to our mononational students who may be mobile within one country and whose education may unfold across different communities in one or more states or regions. If we are dealing with a situation where a transnational student will be returning to our classroom within the same academic year or even to another literacy classroom in our school in a subsequent year, we will create a second section of the academic plan. There, we will draw from our already developed, general curriculum plans to outline the academic work we will be undertaking in our classroom while our transnational students are away. This portion of the plan can take the form of a bulleted list of short sentences that state the kinds of reading, writing, and other learning processes and activities that will be happening, their duration, and any major assignments our students will undertake. We might also list some specific learning activities that we want our transnational students to engage while they are away and some types of texts and learning tools that they can use to develop those academic literacies. That section of the plan could look something like this:

> Below is an outline of the academic work we will be completing while Monica is learning with you and your students:
>
> - January 6–20: Independent Reading Unit. Students will choose a book they are interested in and read it during and outside class. They will keep a reader's notebook and write in it every day about their thinking about the book and what they find enjoyable and hard about reading the book.

- January 21–30: Whole-class text. We will choose one book to read as a whole class and we will read the book both in and out of class. Our major learning goal is to build our skills at having productive conversations with one another about texts. The major assignment is for students to write a paper about how they developed their skills of participating in classroom conversation and what they learned from reading and discussing a book with their classmates.
- February 1–March 15: We will be doing a writing unit and focusing on feature articles. We will read and study many examples of this kind of writing from magazines and other sources. We will practice the craft of feature writing. Students will keep a writer's notebook to write what they are learning about the genre of feature writing, brainstorm ideas for a feature article, and work on drafts of a feature article. For the major assignment, students will compose their own feature article. We will compile our articles into a class magazine that we will circulate among our school and community.

Below are some ideas to help Monica keep working on the academic skills we are developing in our class:

- Monica has already chosen some books from our classroom library to bring with her to St. Maarten. She can also choose some new books that interest her from her new school or public library.
- Monica has agreed to continue reading every day and writing in her reader's notebook. She will talk about her reading with her mother. Monica has also agreed to find two or more friends with whom she will talk weekly about the books they are reading.
- Monica and I have talked about the feature article writing unit. Monica likes feature articles on travel. I have given her several articles on feature writing and asked her to collect as many as she can (from airplane magazines or tourism offices in St. Maarten and St. Martin). Monica will use her writer's notebook to try writing feature articles.

Of course, the intention of this academic plan is not to replace our fellow transnational teacher's curriculum. Rather, its purpose is to develop our colleagues' awareness of the competencies that our students possess and need to strengthen if they are going to be successful in their new classroom and to help ease students' re-entry and success in our classroom. Because we acknowledge that the teachers receiving our transnational students cannot reasonably allow our students to pursue an entirely different curriculum in their classrooms, the academic plan I invented suggested some outside-school spaces, such as home and social spaces with friends, in which Monica can pursue this academic learning. I also suggested some academic scaffolds or activities that Monica and her family can use to augment her academic learning such as regular reading, writing, and talking about texts and experimenting with new and more complex forms of writing. In ways such as this, we would want to recruit the help of our transnational teacher colleagues (as well as our students themselves and their families) in assisting and encouraging the student to continue building the academic literacies we have articulated in the plan.

This type of academic plan will work best if it is developed collaboratively. If we, as teachers who currently have the transnational students, originate the plan, we should try to consult with the students and their families to create a plan that everyone thinks is important, relevant, useful, and doable. We can also ask our students and their families to write some parts of the academic plan. For example, students can write the introductory portion that describes their personalities, social and literate interests, and learning styles in and out of the classroom. They can describe the different cultures and languages they identify with and know well, the languages in which they are fluent and the ones they are still learning, and in what ways they think their cultural and language skills will help them be successful in their new school. Beginning back in Chapter 2, we have seen how this kind of exploring and sharing about one's literate self is a worthy academic assignment for all students as they enter a new classroom.

If we actually have contact with the teachers who will be receiving our transnational students, we would want to seek their input, for instance, by emailing them a draft of the plan. Language differences between us and our transnational teacher colleagues can be addressed by asking students, families, or community members to help translate the plan into the target language or by using translation tools and other linguistic resources, like those available on the Internet, with care. Codeveloping or consulting about this academic plan will enable everyone involved to notice the ways in which academic work in TC 1 and TC 2 does and does not align and come up with ideas for how our teaching can capitalize on similarities and bridge any gaps. Whether or not it is possible to collaborate on this plan with the pertinent transnational teachers, the main point is to share it with them, even if that sharing occurs through our students hand delivering those plans to their new teachers when they arrive in those classrooms.

Figure 4.1 lists the major components of an academic plan.

Figure 4.1. Components of an Academic Plan

- A description of academic, social, cultural, linguistic, and other strengths the student already possesses that will support his or her success in school in the other context.
- A description of the academic, social, linguistic or other challenges the student may face and some ideas of how teachers might support the student in those areas.
- A description of the specific academic work the teacher and students will be undertaking while the student is away.
- A list of reading and writing tasks and other learning activities that the student can engage with while he or she is away to stay abreast of the class.

TEACHING ACROSS TRANSNATIONAL SCHOOL SETTINGS BEYOND TRANSITION

Having completed the work of transition, we will want to stay updated on how learning is proceeding for our transnational students in literacy classrooms or schools in their other nations. Although we will not be teaching these students during that period in the sense of daily curricular and instructional interactions, we do want to continue thinking of ourselves as these young people's current and active teachers. If we stay abreast of the teaching and learning that our transnational, or other, students are experiencing in other classrooms, it will help us smooth these students' transitions back into our literacy classrooms. Even if we do not expect these students to return to our classrooms during the same school year, or at all, we can still serve as a source of academic support for them. Indeed, our transnational students may see us as an especially valuable academic resource, particularly if we are the first of their teachers to have made their transnational lives a significant component of their literacy education. Furthermore, our transnational students' sojourns in other countries create avenues to explore potential curricular bridges across our classrooms and other transnational learning environments. We'll wrap up this chapter by exploring some strategies and activities we can use to stay informed about our students' educational lives in other countries. These approaches will also help us stay abreast of the educational lives of any of the students who leave our classrooms, whether or not they have immediate plans to return to us. Finally, we'll explore a unique curricular idea that can be engaged across transnational school settings.

Documenting and Sharing Teaching and Learning Experiences

Educational activities and academic learning are documentable practices and processes. Our students, their families, and we, as teachers, can record teaching and learning, and there are a number of tools and strategies we can use to do so. We can ask our transnational students, or any of our students who will be attending other schools for a time, to keep a learning journal. In this journal, students will write every few days about how learning is proceeding for them, what curriculum and instructional approaches and learning activities are working well, and which are difficult. Students can also write about what they, their teachers, their families, and others are doing, or can do, to support their learning. We can also ask students to create a portfolio in which they file significant academic work that they complete during a semester or whatever time period they are away from our classroom. Our students and their families can also ask one or more of the students' current teachers in the other country to write a short description or summary about the students' learning experiences in their classrooms—areas of growth and challenge—to be shared with us, teachers who are also involved in the education of these youths.

Teachers, students, and families would also need to identify some ways to share these kinds of information, and more generally, our strategies for staying in touch. One possible way to stay abreast of developments is via bimonthly emails—for instance, in which we share a list of major learning activities and objectives each of us has accomplished. If our students are keeping learning journals, they can share those at agreed-upon points in time with the two (or more) teachers involved across TC 1 and TC 2. This sharing can happen through digital means, as available. All the transnational youths with whom I have worked, and transnational youths in other research studies (e.g., Lam & Rosario-Ramos, 2009; Lam & Warriner, 2012; Skerrett, 2012a), confirm that they rely heavily on the Internet and digital literacies to stay connected with the people in their lives across transnational locations. Except in geographic regions and economic circumstances that do not allow those digital affordances, we can feel confident suggesting that our students stay in touch with us through the Internet and other digital means. If we and our students are not able to keep regular communications, at a minimum, we will ask our students to return to us with some oral or written report or tangible examples of the major learning experiences, growth, and challenges they experienced in a transnational school or other educational setting. These data will be critically useful as we devise an instructional approach for reintegrating students into our classroom learning communities.

Stretching Inquiry Units Across Transnational School Contexts

It may seem idealistic to consider innovations of collaborative teaching with transnational teacher colleagues given our newness to transnational education. Yet, this book, in positioning transnationalism as a resource for literacy education, compels us to consider such possibilities. Our transnational students can experience a form of literacy education in which learning flows across borders. Travel back and forth provides exciting opportunities for students to carry inquiry questions across national borders. If our students have been interested in a particular question about transnational life (one they may have posed during the process of becoming transnationally literate that we explored in Chapter 2 or that they have taken on in a critical inquiry project like the kind we examined in Chapter 3), time spent in each context becomes an opportunity to research those topics actively. For instance, if students have been looking at differences in school funding or educational options across the countries in which they are educated (topics that Monica and Sasha were highly knowledgeable and critically aware of), or migration flows and related social and political sentiments across their countries of habitation, they can capitalize on extended time in each context to interview informants and read a variety of local documents that can help answer their questions.

If this inquiry assignment originated in our classroom, when our students return to us we can count such an inquiry as evidence of learning and documentation of our students' academic engagement and development while they were away. If we have established some relationship and dialogue around literacy teaching and learning with our transnational teacher colleagues, we may wish to consider together whether and how this inquiry can count as official schoolwork in our transnational colleagues' classrooms. Just about any inquiry a student conducts will require substantive and careful reading, writing, or other composing practices, as well as thoughtful analysis. These competencies appear across the literacy curricula of many nations. Students and teachers who build those skills transnationally are curriculum innovators and should be regarded quite favorably.

CHAPTER 5

Sponsoring Students' Literate Lives Across Nonschool Transnational Settings

We have just examined a number of ways through which we can support our transnational students' academic development in schools in other countries. This chapter is especially concerned with our transnational students who do not enroll in formal schools during their time in another nation. We will delve into the spaces of transnational youths' literate lives that lie outside formal school settings to make ourselves more aware of the valuable language and literacy learning opportunities that exist in students' literate activities in nonschool spaces. We will learn how we can use what we discover about our transnational students' outside-school literate lives to help them strengthen their language and literacy repertoires. It is important to provide this assistance to our transnational students, who spend lengthy periods of time away from us, as well as to our mononational students. Both our transnational and mononational students spend several summer months away from school and many more hours each week outside our classrooms than they spend inside them. Thus, the outside-school literate lives of all our students present us with substantial opportunities to support their literacy development.

We should equip our students to take greatest advantage of their outside-school language and literacy learning opportunities. Teaching students honorably includes supporting their pursuit of the literate activities, learning, and goals that matter to them beyond those that the school curriculum has selected. However, we also know that young people, in their literate lives beyond school, are already engaging with many of the kinds of reading, writing, and social and cognitive processes that we teach them in academic settings (Christenbury, Bomer, & Smagorinsky, 2009; Skerrett & Bomer, 2011, 2013). We can be confident that as we support our students' outside-school literate lives, we are also naturally supporting their development of the literacies that matter in academic settings. This understanding is particularly important in the case of transnational students who do not engage in formal schooling in one of their homelands. As these transnational youths prepare to leave our classrooms, we can encourage and plan with them to engage with their nonschool activities as literate processes and practices in which they, as individuals and in community with others, use and strengthen important capacities as readers, writers, thinkers, and producers of valuable literacy artifacts.

You already met Cameron at the beginning of the book. We'll hear more now from this young man's story of music literacy education across formal and informal, school and nonschool, spaces across the transnational settings of French St. Martin, Dutch St. Maarten, and New York City. Cameron's narrative compellingly portrays transnational and other youths' rich literate lives both in and outside of school settings. Next, we will survey a variety of formal and informal spaces outside of school in which young people, and, in particular, transnational youths, participate and develop their multiliterate, multilingual, and multicultural repertoires. We will then review some of the instructional approaches we explored in Chapter 2 and explore some new ideas for identifying and learning about the many outside-school contexts of language and literacy in which our students participate. We will also learn how to design what I call a Plan for Literate Engagement with our students. This plan presents a comprehensive approach through which we can help our transnational as well as mononational students purposefully build and wield their language and literacy repertoires in outside-school literacy contexts beyond our physical reach. Finally, we will consider how transnational and other students can undertake a self-directed inquiry project in outside-school contexts on a topic that is significant to them.

TRANSNATIONAL LITERACY SPACES OF CAMERON'S LIFE

Cameron enjoyed a vibrant musical literate life. Throughout his early childhood and adolescent years on St. Martin, Cameron's family provided extensive music training for him, augmenting the music education he received throughout the school grades that was part of the island's official curriculum. Cameron explained:

> In kindergarten we took music courses and sang songs and stuff. And then when I got into primary school—every school that I have been to had music, a time for music, and we sang. And then my dad took me to a music school on the French side [St. Martin] where I can't remember what I played, but I was very young. And then we had our first little concert, and I played. I can't remember what I played but yes, it was fun. And that's when I think I got really attached to music.

Cameron's musical life was also deeply connected to his family's transnational involvement in the arts.

> I have a cousin in St. Martin. And her sisters, they all sing in different talent shows here, and they sing also Calypso music. My cousin won a lot of Calypso crowns [traditional Calypso music competitions in the Caribbean where the winner is "crowned" as Calypso King for that year]. I have a

> cousin and I can't remember where she lives—they live somewhere in New York, and she was on Broadway. And she was in a Tyler Perry movie also, *For Colored Girls.*

During his annual visits to New York, Cameron developed an expansive view of the possibilities for developing his musical talents in different social spaces in that city: professional performing arts events, a performing arts academy that his mother attended for high school, and a variety of churches. He told me how he, his mother, and other family members would "go to different shows . . . choirs, choir shows" and "plays [and] musicals," and how, "since my mom was also in the choir and she was in high school in New York, she had me visit where she went to school. And they had like a big show and everything." These transnational experiences with music, in and outside school, and across formal and informal literate spaces, led Cameron to conclude that the music world of New York City "was much bigger than what I saw here in St. Martin." And, at the end of his 9th grade year in St. Martin, Cameron decided to complete high school at his mother's alma mater, the performing arts school in New York City.

The following year, Cameron moved in with his aunt in New York City to attend this school. His aunt "took me to my first class . . . [which] was Chorus class" and announced to the teacher, "this young man, he is a very good singer." The year before Cameron arrived, the teacher had introduced Show Choir to the school, a performing arts genre "where you sing and dance at the same time while portraying a story." The teacher asked Cameron "to audition. . . . Yeah, she asked me to sing the U.S. National Anthem, and I did. And she was blown away. That's what she told me. And she immediately put me on to be a part of show choir."

FORMAL NONSCHOOL SPACES OF LITERATE LIFE

Formal literacy spaces outside of school will be as diverse as the identities and interests, family situations, and cultural socializations of any group of youths. Because Cameron's family was heavily involved in the arts, they prioritized formal voice and instrument training for him from the time he was 4 until age 14 when he moved to New York City. Cameron first experienced group lessons in small music programs run by people at his church, a cousin, and other community members, then progressed to individual instruction at age 9. He recalled an initial dislike for private lessons that, over time, shifted to appreciation as his development as a musician accelerated as a result of personalized lessons.

> I didn't like the [music class] that I moved to at 9. I didn't really like it . . . 'cause I thought it was kind of a downgrade. That it was more fun to be with everyone. But then I realized it's, it takes more time when you are with a bunch of people with different instruments, instead of, rather than being

> by yourself with the teacher. You learn more. And you understand better. . . . And then eventually after you learn whatever piece you need to learn, that's when he [the teacher] brings in each piece. And it comes together as a band.

Churches, temples, mosques, and other formal religious organizations are important places for transnational and other youths to learn to read, interpret, and compose according to particular religious and cultural beliefs and traditions, and using particular languages and literacy practices that they are not typically invited to engage in school (Dallavis, 2011; Juzwik, 2014; Sarroub, 2002; Skerrett, 2014; Wallace, 2008). The literacies in formal religious settings include multimodal ways of making meaning—singing, playing musical instruments, dance, and drama performance: multiliteracies that Cameron further developed through participating in religious contexts. Cameron described the centrality of church and other formal settings in building his music literacies. He told me how he was "raised in church" where he sang in the choir and for special concert events and also gave solo performances.

Being involved with music and church opened significant literate opportunities for Cameron.

> When I started in church, people heard about me, and out of church also. And I really had different events and concerts, [but] I still sang in church. I never really stopped singing in church. Yeah, the first time I performed the St. Martin song [akin to the National Anthem] was for a big [national event]. And I was asked to do it, and I practiced for days. It was really my first time singing for a big event. I think I was 7. And it went pretty well. And after that it just went on from there. I got more gigs, more places to sing.

One of those gigs was being "a cohost on the gospel program on the gospel station in St. Martin," something Cameron did "off and on for about 5 years" from the time "they approached me like when I was 8." Cameron thought the radio programmers offered him this role because "they thought I was brave because singers are brave because they stand in front of an audience. So they came to me and asked me if I would like to be part of the show. Of course, I agreed." Importantly, then, Cameron's singing and instrument playing led him to develop other literacies on this media program, a formal outside-school institution, involving oral performances of Bible stories, where "we had like different parts and we would tell the story." Cameron also identified other literacies he wanted to build as he engaged with music and the performing arts. For instance, Cameron wanted to get better at writing music. He told me how "I always try to write, but I never excelled at it. So I sang different types of songs . . . songs I like, songs that people asked me to sing."

Beyond multiliteracies, literacy researchers have learned that religious life is also an important space for students to explore and further develop their cultural identities (Dallavis, 2011; Sarroub, 2002; Skerrett, 2014). Additionally, students whose home language is different from the official language of their school(s) and the broader societ(ies) in which they live are sometimes able to maintain and build their home language, and also add new ones, by participating in formal religious settings (Owodally, 2011; Wallace, 2008). We have seen how both Cameron and Sasha (in the previous chapter) pursued music through interconnected formal literacy settings—music school, church, and the typical educational setting of school—across transnational life. Moving across transnational settings allowed these youths to engage with music in different languages—English, French, and Dutch—and the distinctive cultures that accompanied each language and literacy setting.

A place of employment is another obvious formal nonschool literacy context. Transnational youths and their families work in an assortment of economic enterprises across nations (Zúñiga & Hamann, 2009). They may work in national and multinational companies that involve the manufacturing and distribution of a plethora of goods and services. They can be self-employed or work within family and local small businesses that make or provide sundry services and goods related to technology; child, home, and beauty care; and food and entertainment. Working in these spaces, transnational youths grow in their knowledge and skills with the particular language, cultural, and literacy practices necessary for successful participation.

On a visit to Monterrey, Mexico, in 2008, my husband and I sat in a Mexican restaurant trying to make sense of the menu that was written in Spanish with the young Mexican woman who was our server. Realizing that our difficulties communicating across language differences were not likely to be overcome at a speed that would allow her to keep working and us to eat, she went off in search of a different server, one we assumed spoke English. The young woman she returned with nodded and smiled at the situation before her—one she likely came across often in her work. She began talking with us in American-accented English, leading my husband to blurt out what we were both thinking: "Are you American? You speak English like an American!" The young woman shared that she had lived and gone to school in Arizona but was living with her family in Monterrey at the time. The point, then, is that this young woman was finding significant ways to use and develop both her Spanish and English in her place of employment in ways that were strengthening her entire linguistic repertoire and serving as an asset to the business as well. When I visited Monica on Dutch St. Maarten in the spring of 2014, I learned that she, too, had landed a job as a cash manager and server in a restaurant in the bustling downtown area of Philipsburg. This restaurant catered to locals and tourists who wanted their meals made with organic Caribbean produce. In her work, Monica strategically drew upon her cultural and linguistic American identities when interacting with American tourists while also signaling her Caribbean identity by switching to a locally accented English to interact with local patrons and coworkers.

INFORMAL NONSCHOOL SPACES OF LITERATE LIFE

Young people participate every day in activities and conversations with other youths and adults at home, in online worlds, in community spaces, on neighborhood street corners. Whether our students lead mononational or transnational lives, they are part of affinity groups (Gee, 2007) in which they and others engage in some shared beloved activity—playing rounders or cricket; fixing cars; composing and performing music like others do in formal spaces; styling hair, faces, and bodies. Cameron, for instance, pointed to an affinity group that is woven into the cultural identity of West Indian girls (a legacy of British colonialism): "My mom had friends, she played with the Rounders Team. . . . They had a tournament in Dominica, and I went with her." Thinking back to Vanesa's literate life, which we explored in Chapter 2, we will recall how Vanesa, her younger sister, and her mother developed an affinity group that was held together by their mutual passion for making art.

We have already seen how transnational youths capitalize on digital literacies to maintain and deepen transnational relationships by creating virtually connected transnational communities (Lam, 2004, 2006; Lam & Rosario-Ramos, 2009). We learned that these virtual communities provide transnational youths with space, activities, and tools to develop their transcultural, multilingual, and multiliterate practices because they share and build these knowledge and skill sets with one another in online worlds. Cameron, for example, used Facebook as a way to create a multilingual (French, English, and Dutch) community of friends and family spread across New York, St. Martin, St. Maarten, and other countries. In that digital transnational space, Cameron wrote about his music successes, setbacks, and goals, and uploaded pictures and videos of his music performances on which he could receive praise, encouragement, and thoughtful critique from friends and family across transnational life. Furthermore, and very importantly, Cameron used Facebook as a marketing tool that provided a vibrant portfolio of his musical talents for a professional audience that could become interested in working with him.

INSTRUCTIONAL APPROACHES FOR LEARNING ABOUT AND SPONSORING STUDENTS' OUTSIDE-SCHOOL LITERATE LIVES

We can rely on approaches similar to those we explored in Chapter 2 for learning about the outside-school literacy spaces in our transnational and mononational students' lives. As a quick review, we studied approaches that involved the following:

- Self-portraiture, an assignment with a short prompt and guiding questions and suggestions that allows students to name and describe

their personal, cultural, and national backgrounds and their language and literacy practices—including the spaces, relationships, tools, processes, and outcomes of their language and literacy activities
- Student inquiries into their individual language practices across social contexts (supported, for instance, by the language study chart designed in Chapter 2), or individual or group inquiries into the language practices of different social groups and communities of which students are a part—their families, their schools, and their local and transnational communities. I suggested that students use interviews, surveys, observations of social settings, and collection and analysis of language and literacy artifacts to conduct these inquiries
- A whole-class inquiry into literate lives like the one Molly Campbell did in her classroom in Austin, Texas, so that she and her students would know more fully the literate identities, knowledge, and skills available in their classroom community

The Literacy Practices Record

We can have students undertake an individual (rather than whole-class) inquiry into their literacy practices by adapting the language study chart (from Chapter 2) into a literacy practices record or, as I have named it for my students, a literacy log. This instructional idea emerged for me after reading Bean, Bean, and Bean (1999). Carried out as an independent activity, this tool will help all our students, regardless of transnational status, notice and document the many facets of their literate lives. Students can keep a literacy log for a week or 2 in which they list and describe the different social activities and contexts in which they participate. The log can include a number of columns that ask for different kinds of information:

- The different activities a student participates in
- The length of time and frequency of each activity
- The language and literacy tools used in each activity (e.g., Spanish, Frenglish, art supplies, guitar, iPods)
- The goals or products of these activities (pleasure, relationships, digital stories)
- The people with whom they participate in those spaces and activities (individual, friends in my neighborhood, siblings)
- The processes or habits of participation (individual reading and reflection, collaborative writing, multimodal performance)

When I teach my adolescent literacy course at the university, I always give the literacy log assignment to my students, who are pre- and inservice English teachers. The adolescent literacy course helps the teacher candidates and practicing teachers develop knowledge about adolescents' multiple literacy practices and instructional strategies they can use to create bridges among the literacy knowledge and skills adolescents engage in outside-school contexts and the academic literacies youths need for school. My university students enjoy the literacy log assignment immensely and it helps reorient their thinking about themselves and their middle and high school students as multiliterate people who do important things with language and literacy all day, every day. Invariably, these pre- and inservice teachers assign the literacy log activity to their own middle and high school students with great success. I have included below two iterations of the literacy log that I created and used with my university students. Although the logs don't capture all of the ideas about literacy practice in the bulleted list above, you will see that the directions for completing the assignments still orient students toward thinking about literacy as social practice. The instructional conversation and written guidelines that frame the assignments enable my students and me to analyze the data they collect on their literate lives in ways that achieve the learning I want my students to experience. I also give my students the option of using a hard copy or electronic version of the logs. Some students, perhaps those who are disposed to being concise, keep their logs on the physical piece of paper. Others prefer to use an electronic version because they can write more freely and fully in that format.

Figure 5.1 is the early iteration of the literacy log assignment I created and used with my university students in the adolescent literacy course. You will notice that I created very distinct categories of literacy practices and even named the forms of literacy practice that I knew to be salient in young people's lives. Notice, though, that I also instructed my students in the introductory directions to modify or jettison everything on the chart if they wished and create something they felt would work better for them. Figure 5.2, a newer version of the literacy log for the same course, shows how I tried to simplify the log. I gave my students more freedom to identify and track the literacy practices that were significant for them, including giving them the option of creating their own categories. Some of my students like the clear categories and tight guidance of the earlier log; others prefer the freedom offered in the later log to name their own significant literacies and create their own categories or ways of tracking and recording their literate lives.

If any kind of chart still feels too restrictive, another idea would be to supply students with a list of questions that get at the different dimensions of literate activity in the bulleted list above and ask them to keep note of their literate activities in a writer's notebook. This more open approach can also take the form of a standing journal entry assignment where, for each day for a week or 2, students write a journal entry reflecting on the people with whom they have spent their day; what specific activities they were involved in; what useful or new information, ideas, or skills they think they acquired from these activities; and how they saw "literacy" manifest in their activities that day. We would want to create periodic opportunities for students to discuss their discoveries and thinking with one another. Students can prepare to talk about their literate lives using the bulleted dimensions of literate life above, which we can provide them as an organizing frame. We would facilitate those conversations by asking probing questions specifically related to what students share. For example:

Figure 5.1. Adolescent Literacy Log Assignment, Version One

This is an exercise to help raise your awareness that we use multiple forms of literacy each day; that we use literacy for academic, social, civic, personal, and other reasons; and that on any given day, our types and degrees of use of particular literacy practices reflect, and help us navigate, the various contexts in which we live our lives.

Choose 3 days out of the next 7 days (1 of the 3 days should be a weekend day) during which you will keep a record of the different ways you access information and communicate with others—for example, through reading traditional printed texts, signs, symbols, and so on; through writing; talking on the phone; texting; listening to or playing music; and any other means through which you receive and transmit information. Also, record the amount of time you spend on each type of literacy practice.

You can use the chart below, adapted from Bean, Bean, and Bean (1999). You can further adapt the chart to better reflect your uses of literacy or create a completely new one of your own.

Self-Observation Tally **Name:** ______________________

Directions: Write in the number of minutes or hours you spend in each suggested category (modify the chart as needed) for 3 days—2 weekdays and 1 weekend day.

Day (Fill in below)	Academic Reading & Writing—Print Form	Personal Informational—Print literacy (e.g., reading road signs, novels, grocery shopping)	Academic Internet, PC Use	Personal PC or Internet Use (email, blogging, Facebook, and so forth)	Phone Use—Talking	Phone Use—Texting	Music	TV, Movies	Videogames/ other media	Other	Multitasking (specify combinations of tasks & amount of time)

Source: Adapted from Bean, Bean, & Bean, 1999

Figure 5.2. Adolescent Literacy Log Assignment, Version Two

LITERACY LOG ASSIGNMENT VERSION TWO

This is an exercise to help raise your awareness that literacy involves making and sharing meaning through various modalities (forms). These modalities include oral language, other sounds, gestures and other forms of body language, print and electronic texts, images, and social spaces that we "read," interpret, and use each day. We use multiple forms of literacy each day; we use literacy for academic, social, civic, personal, and other purposes; and the types and amounts of literacy practices in which we engage each day reflect the different responsibilities, interests, and opportunities afforded by each day.

Directions: On the chart on the next page, fill in your daily activities and the amount of time (minutes or hours) you spend on each activity. Some activities students usually record include: academic reading of print and online materials, academic writing such as note taking in class or writing essays, personal reading of print materials, surfing the web for different kinds of information, email, blogging, Facebook, face to face interactions, texting or talking on the phone, playing videogames, watching movies or television shows, listening to music, cooking, shopping, playing sports, doing various hobbies, performing job duties, and driving.

Do this for three days—two weekdays and one weekend day.

An electronic version of this form is on Blackboard. You can modify it as needed or create a new chart of your own. You can also use an online tool such as http://www.readwritethink.org/files/resources/interactives/timeline/ and www.dipity.com.

(continued)

Figure 5.2. Adolescent Literacy Log Assignment, Version Two *(continued)*

LITERACY LOG

Name: ____________________

Day 1 ____________	Day 2 ____________	Day 3 ____________
List activities & duration in rows below	*List activities & duration in rows below*	*List activities & duration in rows below*

- What other tools do you use in your artwork and how do you use them?
- What is the role of reading, writing, and languages in these practices and settings you talked about?
- What products do you create in these activities or with this group of people? How are those things important to you or other people?
- What do you enjoy best about working at this job? About playing soccer with this group of people in a particular country?
- How is worshipping at your church in one country different from another and why do you think that is?

Multiliteracies Documentations of Literate Life

With handheld devices that allow immediacy and convenience in writing and audio- and video-recording, a literacy log assignment can become an opportunity for students to create real-time records of what they are doing with literacy across the hours of their days. Another idea, then, is to encourage students to use audio- or video-recordings on their cellphones or other technologies to help them document their literate lives. In my research, youth participants like Vanesa were given disposable cameras to take pictures of significant things, people, events, and places in their lives that held some literate importance for them. The youths also enjoyed bringing us artifacts that represented their literate lives—artwork, videos of dance recordings, stories they had written, religious symbols from their home. Imagine the richness of the displays and conversations that would manifest in our classrooms as our students presented photographs and artifacts from their literate lives!

A Plan for Literate Engagement

As our transnational students prepare to leave us for another country, we can return to the data they have collected on their outside-school literate lives through one or another of the assignments above to remind ourselves of the formal and informal literate spaces and activities in which they participate in outside-school transnational settings. We will be thinking specifically about the opportunities for language and literacy development that are available for them in those spaces and activities outside of school. From these data, we can work with our students to develop a plan that will help them engage with their outside-school literate lives in ways that produce enjoyment and growth in a range of language and literacy practices. This plan is especially critical for our transnational students who will not enroll in a formal school setting during their stay in a particular country. It is, however, also vital for all of our transnational youths—and indeed, for all of our students—who have whole literate lives of which formal schools are just a small part. This Plan for Literate Engagement is something we can develop with all our students to support their literacy development outside school. For example, we can integrate this activity into end-of-year units before summer vacation or the weeks preceding an extended school break, sending our students off with concrete plans and strategies for growing their literacies while they are away from school. Such a robust and innovative plan is sure to be received by students and their families with interest and eagerness, as a welcome addition to, or departure from, the stock summer assignment of a school-selected list of books to read.

Below, I design and take us through this three-part Plan for Literate Engagement. The sections of this plan are: (1) Description of Outside-School Literate Life, (2) Goals and Related Activities for Literacy Participation and Development, and (3) Artifacts from Literate Life. These elements are broad and flexible enough to provide direction and support for students' development across many social contexts and forms of language and literacy practice. Because the literacies of reading and writing are significant in many domains of life, I also include in this plan some ways to encourage students to build their habits and skills in reading and writing in any contexts and activities of literate life they engage with outside of school. In working out this plan, I imagined that Cameron is one of my transnational students. However, because he is not, and because I cannot draw from a school assignment he completed on his literate life, I draw instead on interview data in which Cameron offered information pertinent to filling out this plan.

Part One: Description of Outside-School Literate Life. The first part of this plan comprises a brief narrative description or a set of short descriptive phrases or sentences that illustrate the student's significant literate activities outside of school. This information will be readily available from the literacy practices record assignment or another assignment that students complete to inquire into their literate lives. First, we would define the dimensions of students' literacy practices with the terms from the literacy practices record such as tools and activities, processes, artifacts, and how reading, writing, and language repertoires are at work. This opening description will provide a framework for the particular goals, activities, and products we will outline in the remaining sections of the plan for supporting students' literacy development in nonschool transnational or mononational contexts. Here is an example of what part one of Cameron's plan might look like:

- Significant activities and spaces of literate life that can or will be engaged outside school:

Singing and playing musical instruments on my own, at home with my family, at church, in formal music lessons, and at special events where I get invited to perform

- Language and literacy tools used in these activities:

Singing in English at home and at church. Music classes are in English and are mostly on voice, piano, and keyboard. I also use the guitar and drums.

- The special processes or forms of participation that comprise those activities, including people and relationships:

When I am by myself, I practice singing my favorite songs and mixing in my own styles or ideas. [I] used to try writing my own songs but found it really hard to do and haven't tried to do that for a while. Family will sometimes sing together at home and if cousins or other family members that sing come over. Somebody will play the piano or keyboard or guitar. Music class involves learning how to read music, perform it exactly, and practice different small parts over and over again with the teacher and on my own. At church, I'm part of a group called the worship team that has a worship director. We practice two or three times a week. There's Sunday morning and evening church services where the worship team leads the congregation but everyone in church sings and dances all together.

- The purposes, goals, or products of these activities:

A love for music. To have fun, feel good, and express myself. An important skill that I'm good at. Opportunities to share with others and use my talents. Would like to be a professional singer for a career. I have CDs and videos of my singing—at big public events and at church in St. Martin and St. Maarten, and in school state competitions in New York. Music performances were broadcasted on the radio in St. Martin and on TV in New York. I was interviewed by CNN about my singing.

Part Two: Goals and Related Activities for Literacy Participation and Development. In this section, students articulate some goals they have for engaging and getting stronger at their literacy practices. We would also work with them to suggest additional goals that they and we agree are important for their growth as literate people and as users of language in a multilingual world. Additionally, we would want to identify some useful activities through which students can pursue and achieve their language and literacy objectives. These activities should be closely tied to the spaces and forms of literate life in which students engage. This list of goals and activities will provide an immediate source of guidance and redirection for students about how to participate productively in literate life to achieve the goals that matter to them.

In articulating literate goals and activities, we can foreground for our students the usefulness of reading and writing and language repertoires. Writing this plan with one of our transnational students, for instance, we might learn that the student will have opportunity to use the language of our school, which he is learning, in one other key site in his other country, such as a work setting. With that student, we would then set a goal of continuing to build his capacities in the language of our school at his workplace—for instance, by conducting work-related reading, writing, and conversation in that language. We would also encourage multilingual transnational youths, and indeed all our multilingual students, to identify how some literate activities they enjoy can provide ways to hold on to their languages—for example, social networking online, writing in a journal, reading books, or watching movies in their different languages. A transnational student for whom religion is a salient part of literate life can choose to keep a special journal detailing how his religious life is unfolding across two or more transnational contexts. We can suggest that the student maintain a dialogue journal about this question with one or more friends or spiritual leaders across TC 1 and TC 2, and encourage multilingual writing if doing so is relevant in a given situation.

Imagining that Cameron was leaving New York for St. Martin, I created some probable goals, with related activities, that he might generate with my help or with the help of another teacher who is knowledgeable about his literate life:

- Re-enroll in music school when I get back to St. Martin with a focus on improving vocal and piano performance
- Try playing piano and keyboard while singing more difficult songs
- Get back on the worship team at my church and share some things I have been learning about music in school in New York
- Stay in touch via email, Google Hangout, or other means with my music teacher in New York for mentorship and to share my progress and get feedback
- Seek out information (from local musicians, local media sources, and so on) about upcoming performing arts events that I can perform in

As his teacher, I could make the following suggestions to Cameron targeted toward developing his reading, writing, and language repertoires:

- Explore writing song lyrics and putting them to music because he has identified this as a part of musical life that is interesting and challenging for him. I see this activity as a further opportunity for Cameron to develop his writing abilities and identity within a literacy activity that is highly significant for him.
    - ➤ Find and study mentor texts
    - ➤ Find and study books/articles/interviews and other sources of information about song writing—for example, in the local library and on the Internet
    - ➤ Seek out a local songwriter to serve as a mentor (ask music teacher or local musicians for potential mentors) or look for mentorship online
    - ➤ Use your writer's notebook to develop ideas and drafts of songs and to reflect on what you are learning about composing music
    - ➤ Find one or two writing partners and make time to read and discuss one another's work and write together
    - ➤ Share and get feedback on your work from friends, family, and others in music networks, including on digital networks

- Include French and Frenglish in music activities in which he typically only uses English—performing, conversing, reading, and writing—as a way to strengthen his French in a context where those language opportunities are more abundant than in the New York contexts in which he lives.
- Keep up with his language journal, focusing on how he is using and thinking about English and French in his music life and other areas of life during his time in St. Martin.
- Keep a music journal to document and reflect on his music practices and development in St. Martin and to connect and compare them to his music life in New York.

Part Three: Artifacts from Literate Life. The third part of the plan contains a list of possible tools and products that our students expect they will use or produce to document how they have pursued and achieved their literacy goals. This list will serve as a source of guidance for students as they become leaders of their own literacy development. One other instructional benefit for students and us is that students will be well equipped to show us and others how they grew as users of languages and literacies in outside-school contexts within one country (in the case of our mononational students) and across national geographies (in the case of our transnational students). Below is a list of tools and products that Cameron could use and produce to document and display his literate engagements and growth:

- Create a portfolio that documents my participation in music literate life and that includes things such as:
  - My writer's notebook
  - My music journal
  - My language journal
  - Examples of texts I read, watched, and listened to
  - Drafts and/or polished final versions of songs I wrote or tried to write
  - Photographs, CDs, DVDs, or a list of hotlinks to my music practices and performances
- Give a multimodal presentation to my class in New York when I return from St. Martin drawing from the materials above. Discuss what I have learned and how I have grown as a musician and performer and present my observations about music literacy practices and education across St. Martin and New York.

The Plan for Literate Engagement can easily accommodate any kind of literate life. It privileges students' interests, strengths, and goals and promotes their agency as users of languages and literacies. This plan also offers students opportunities to develop as readers and writers in ways that support the literate lives that matter to them. Students' reading and writing practices within their self-chosen literate activities also help them improve at the literacies that matter most for school and other domains of life. As students add spaces and activities of literate life to their plan, they—along with us, their teachers—will notice multiplying opportunities for students to develop as readers, writers, and users of languages centered on, rather than displacing or diminishing, their valued literacy practices.

Self-Directed, Outside-School Inquiry Project

We have already explored formal research projects or inquiry units a teacher might assign that can be carried across formal school settings in the transnational contexts students inhabit. It is worth considering the feasibility and utility of such a project that a transnational youth could carry on outside of a formal school setting as well. In a related vein, we can plan for all of our students to engage in a self-directed inquiry project based on authentic practices, questions, and goals from their literate lives. For instance, think of transnational or mononational students who identify a family business as a vital place of literacy participation. In the case of transnational youths, living and working across two or more countries introduces an opportunity to undertake their own business inquiry project. This project might involve them in collecting and composing archives of business reports, magazine articles, news stories, and their own written notes to show what they are learning about cross-national opportunities for learning particular knowledge and skills that may benefit that business. Students who live in one country could also pose questions and problems related to the business in which they work, and seek out solutions through the same kinds of research activities. Indeed, given the globalized nature of business, and all domains of life today, it is very possible that an inquiry question posed within a mononational framing will lead a student to relevant information and perspectives from other parts of the world.

If we assign an inquiry project to students to conduct on their own outside of school, we can signal the importance and rigor of this literacy work even more by having it "count" as academic work. Students who undertake such a project would be prepared to create and share a portfolio or a multimodal presentation that displays their literacy engagement and learning in and about an outside-school literacy setting, whether it crosses national borders or remains within the boundaries of one nation. More than just displaying their knowledge, students who carry out serious investigation into aspects of personal, community, economic, or civic life will develop important knowledge, perspectives, and skills that they can apply to improve situations in which they hold a stake. The circumstances of transnational life, and indeed the character of all social life today, create a pressing need for us to facilitate our students' ownership and leadership of their literate lives and their learning both in and outside school. To do this, we must genuinely honor and support our students' development as literate people in the ways that youths—and not just the school curriculum—value.

CHAPTER 6

Conclusion

The Imperatives for and Unique Benefits of Transnational Approaches to Literacy Education

This book has created an approach to literacy education that supports the learning and development of transnational students, as well as their mononational peers who sit alongside them in the classrooms of diverse nations. The book represents one response to the urgent need to develop approaches to literacy education that include and support transnational youths (Hamann et al., 2006; Sánchez, 2007a, 2007b, 2009; Skerrett, 2012a; Zúñiga & Hamann, 2009). A transnationally aware approach to literacy education, like the one designed in this book, is a social justice demand as well as a principled, and surely achievable, professional response on our parts as literacy educators. Rather than offering a "transnational" curriculum and instructional approach that applies narrowly to a particular demographic of our students alone, this book has shown how we can make literacy education more productive and powerful for *all* students by foregrounding transnationalism in the teaching and learning that occurs in our classrooms.

An important tenet of this book has been that teaching mindfully to transnationalism is an international, not a mononational, endeavor. No single teacher and no sole nation is wholly responsible for the education of transnational youths. Thus, in designing a transnational approach to literacy education, I have avoided laying this project at the feet of any one teacher in any one country. Rather, I have highlighted roles and relationships for and with other educational partners—transnational students themselves, their families, and teachers and stakeholders in other countries—in supporting the literacy education of transnational youths both in and outside of formal school settings. Moreover, the instructional approaches, tools, and processes I selected for enacting a transnationally aware approach to literacy education—students' reading, writing, and analyses of multimodal, multilingual, and multicultural/transnational texts, and inquiry into significant social, educational, and political issues—can and should be carried across transnational contexts.

In its purposive attention to the phenomenon of transnational life, this book has illustrated how intentionally engaging with transnationalism can directly ameliorate the unique transnational educational dilemmas with which we are already grappling in our classrooms. We have explored how teaching across transnational educational settings will improve the coherence and continuity of students' literacy education and help ease the harsh educational ruptures that currently mark the educational life of scores of transnational youths. We have also learned how teaching across transnational settings will concurrently support the academic development of transnational youths across contexts and the literacy education of their mononational peers in a single nation. Furthermore, the book has showed us how to engage with transnationalism in order to reap the significant benefits that this phenomenon presents to the literacy education of all our students, regardless of their transnational status.

We began with the premise that teaching with an awareness of, and in response to, transnationalism is theoretically and instructionally aligned with sound approaches to literacy education that recognize, value, and recruit students' cultural, linguistic, and multiliterate repertoires for teaching and learning. Thus, we have built an approach where being aware of transnationalism while teaching adds power to our and our students' pursuit of important literacy learning objectives. As we close this book, however, it is important to re-articulate and re-emphasize the unique and important benefits that can be reaped from attending to transnationalism in literacy education. Teaching and learning with awareness of transnationalism positions us and our students—transnational as well as mononational—to achieve unique knowledge and understandings, dispositions, and capacities that are essential for all people in an increasingly globalized world. These include:

- understandings and appreciation of how transnational students and their repertoires comprise part of the diverse and valuable resources for teaching and learning available in our classrooms;
- understandings and knowledge about the cultural, linguistic, social, educational, economic, and other dimensions of different nations, or particular regions or communities within them, to which our transnational students have ties;
- critical understandings of how transnationalism is a part of each of our lives;
- increasing expertise at noticing, critiquing, caring about, and developing productive strategies to address personal, social, academic, civic, and other challenges that transnational individuals, groups, communities, and societies face;
- in a related vein, a sense of global citizenship;
- capacities to observe and value how all people draw from their knowledge about different social contexts and language and literacy skills to achieve social, educational, political, and other goals in and across transnational settings;
- deeper understandings of cultural and linguistic flexibility as a strength;

- abilities to notice and understand more deeply how each of us uses our language and cultural repertoires and identities to engage with literacy in and out of school; and
- greater knowledge and capacities related to using, growing, combining, and modifying language, cultural, and social repertoires for productive learning and participation in and across transnational literacy contexts.

Foremost in our minds as literacy educators is the fact that our students will become stronger readers, writers, and critical thinkers from employing the phenomenon of transnationalism and its associated resources for academic learning. Our students will develop specialized abilities to read, write, investigate, analyze, interact, think, know, and act in ways that are deeply and critically informed by a transnational standpoint.

References

Anzaldúa, G. (1987). *Borderlands/La frontera: The new mestiza*. San Francisco, CA: Aunt Lute Books.

Apple, M. W. (1979). *Ideology and curriculum*. London, England: Routledge & Kegan Paul.

Apple, M. W. (1993). *Official knowledge: Democratic education in a conservative age*. New York, NY: Routledge.

Applebee, A. N. (1974). *Tradition and reform in the teaching of English: A history*. Urbana, IL: National Council of Teachers of English.

Araujo, B., & de la Piedra, M. T. (2013). Violence on the U.S.-Mexico border and the capital students use in response. *International Journal of Qualitative Studies in Education, 26*(3), 705–721.

Avramidis, K., & Drakopoulou, K. (2012). Graffiti crews' potential pedagogical role. *Journal for Critical Education Policy Studies, 10*(1), 327–340.

Bakhtin, M. M. (1981). *The dialogic imagination* (Trans. M. Holquist & C. Emerson). Austin, TX: University of Texas Press.

Ball, A. F. (2009). Toward a theory of generative change in culturally and linguistically complex classrooms. *American Educational Research Journal 46*(1), 45–72.

Ball, A. F., Skerrett, A., & Martínez, R. A. (2010). Research on diverse students in culturally and linguistically complex language arts classrooms. In D. Lapp & D. Fisher (Eds.), *Handbook of research on teaching the English language arts* (3rd ed., pp. 22–28). New York, NY: Routledge.

Barton, D., Hamilton, M., & Ivanic, R. (Eds.). (2000). *Situated literacies: Reading and writing in context*. London, England: Routledge.

Bean, T. W., Bean, S. K., & Bean, K. F. (1999). Intergenerational conversations and two adolescents' multiple literacies: Implications for redefining content area literacies. *Journal of Adolescent and Adult Literacy, 42*(6), 438–448.

Bernardi, L. (2011). A mixed-method social networks study design for research on transnational families. *Journal of Marriage and Family, 73*(4), 788–803.

Bernstein, B. (1971). On the classification and framing of educational knowledge. In *Class, codes and control. Volume I: Theoretical studies towards a sociology of language* (pp. 202–230). London, England: Routledge & Kegan Paul.

Bhabha, H. K. (1994). *The location of culture*. London, England: Routledge.

Black, R. W. (2005). Access and affiliation: The literacy and composition practices of English-language learners in an online fanfiction community. *Journal of Adolescent and Adult Literacy, 49*(2), 118–128.

Black, R. W. (2009). English-language learners, fan communities, and 21st century skills. *Journal of Adolescent and Adult Literacy, 52*(8), 688–697.

Bledsoe, C. H., & Sow, P. (2011). Back to Africa: Second chances for the children of West African immigrants. *Journal of Marriage and Family, 73*(4), 747–762.

Bomer, R. (2011). *Building adolescent literacy in today's English classrooms.* Portsmouth, NH: Heinemann.

Bruna, K. R. (2007). Traveling tags: The informal literacies of Mexican newcomers in and out of the classroom. *Linguistics and Education, 18*(3–4), 232–257.

Canagarajah, A. S. (2006). The place of world Englishes in composition. Pluralization continued. *College Composition and Communication, 57*(4), 586–619.

Canagarajah, A. S. (2009). The plurilingual tradition and the English language in South Asia. *AILA Review, 22,* 5–22.

Cepal.org. (2002). *The impact of immigration on Caribbean microstates: Bahamas, British Virgin Islands, Saint Maarten, United States Virgin Islands.* Available at www.cepal.org/publicaciones/xml/0/10340/carg0540.pdf

Charmaz, K. (2000). Grounded theory: Objectivist and constructivist methods. In N. Denzin & Y. Lincoln (Eds.), *Handbook of qualitative research* (2nd ed., pp. 509–535). Thousand Oaks, CA: Sage Publications.

Christenbury, L., Bomer, R., & Smagorinsky, P. (2009). *Handbook of adolescent literacy research.* New York, NY: Guilford Press.

Coe, E., Reynolds, R. R., Boehm, D. A., Hess, J. M., & Rae-Espinoza, H. (Eds.) (2011). *Everyday ruptures: Children, youth, and migration in global perspective.* Nashville, TN: Vanderbilt University Press.

Dallavis, C. (2011). "Because that's who I am": Extending theories of culturally responsive pedagogy to consider religious identity, belief, and practice. *Multicultural Perspectives, 13*(3), 138–144.

Damico, J., Baildon, M., Exter, M., & Shiau-Jing, G. (2010). Where we read from matters: Disciplinary literacy in a ninth-grade social studies classroom. *Journal of Adolescent and Adult Literacy, 53*(4), 325–335.

de la Piedra, M. T. (2010). Adolescent worlds and literacy practices on the United States-Mexico border. *Journal of Adolescent & Adult Literacy, 53*(7), 575–584.

Fisher, M. T. (2005). From the coffeehouse to the schoolhouse: The promise and potential of spoken word poetry in schools. *English Education, 37*(2), 115–131.

Franzak, J. K. (2008). On the margins in a high-performing high school: Policy and the struggling reader. *Research in the Teaching of English, 42*(4), 466–505.

Fu, D., & Graff, J. M. (2009). The literacies of new immigrant youth. In L. Christenbury, R. Bomer, & P. Smagorinksy (Eds.), *Handbook of adolescent literacy research* (pp. 400–414). New York, NY: Guilford Press.

García, A., & Gaddes, A. (2012). Weaving language and culture: Latina adolescent writers in an after-school writing project. *Reading & Writing Quarterly: Overcoming Learning Difficulties, 28*(2), 143–163.

Gee, J. P. (1999). *An introduction to discourse analysis: Theory and method.* London, England: Routledge.

Gee, J. P. (2006). Self-fashioning and shape-shifting: Language, identity, and social class. In D. E. Alvermann, K. A. Hinchman, D. W. Moore, S. F. Phelps, & D. W. Raff (Eds.), *Reconceptualizing the literacies in adolescents' lives* (2nd ed., pp. 165–185). Mahwah, NJ: Erlbaum.

Gee, J. P. (2007). *Good video games + good learning: Collected essays on video games, learning, and literacy.* New York, NY: Peter Lang Publishing.

Glaser, B. G., & Strauss, A. L. (2006). *The discovery of grounded theory: Strategies for qualitative research.* Chicago, IL: Aldine Publishing Co.

Gonzalez, N., Moll, L. C., & Amanti, C. (2005). *Funds of knowledge: Theorizing practices in households and classrooms.* Mahwah, NJ: Lawrence Erlbaum Associates.

Government of Sint Maarten. (2014). *SintMaartenGov.org. The official website of the government of Sint Maarten.* Available at www.sintmaartengov.org/Pages/default.aspx

Graham, E., & Jordan, L. P. (2011). Migrant parents and the psychological well-being of left-behind children in South-Asia. *Journal of Marriage and Family, 73*(4), 763–787.

Guerra, J. C. (2007). Out of the valley: Transcultural repositioning as a rhetorical practice in ethnographic research and other aspects of everyday life. In C. Lewis, P. Enciso, & E. B. Moje (Eds.), *Reframing sociocultural research on literacy: Identity, agency, and power* (pp. 137–162). Mahwah, NJ: Erlbaum.

Gutiérrez, K. D. (2008). Developing a sociocritical literacy in the third space. *Reading Research Quarterly, 43*(2), 148–164.

Hamann, E. T. (2001). Theorizing the sojourner student with a sketch of appropriate school responsiveness. In M. C. Hopkins & N. Wellmeier (Eds.), *Negotiating transnationalism: Selected papers on refugees and immigrant*, Vol. IX (pp. 32–71). Arlington, VA: American Anthropology Association.

Hamann, E. T., & Zúñiga, V. A. (2011). Schooling and the everyday ruptures transnational children encounter in the United States and Mexico. In C. Coe, R. R. Reynolds, D. A. Boehm, J. M. Hess, & H. Rae-Espinoza (Eds.), *Everyday ruptures: Children, youth, and migration in global perspective* (pp. 141–160). Nashville, TN: Vanderbilt University Press.

Hamann, E. T., Zúñiga, V., & Sánchez García, J. (2006). Pensando en Cynthia y su hermana: Educational implications of United States-Mexico transnationalism for children. *Journal of Latinos and Education, 50*(4), 253–274.

Hershberg, R. M., & Lykes, M. B. (2013). Redefining family: Transnational girls narrate experiences of parental migration, detention, and deportation. *FQS: Forum Qualitative Sozialforschung/Forum: Qualitative Research, 14*(1), Art. 5. Available at http://nbn-resolving.de/urn:nbn:de:0114-fqs130157

Jiménez, R. T., Smith, P. H., & Teague, B. L. (2009). Transnational and community literacies for teachers. *Journal of Adolescent and Adult Literacy, 53*(1), 16–26.

Juzwik, M. M. (2014). American evangelical Biblicism as literate practice: A critical review. *Reading Research Quarterly, 49*(3), 335–349.

Kinloch, V. (2009). *Harlem on our minds: Place race and the literacies of urban youth.* New York, NY: Teachers College Press.

Kinloch, V. (Ed.). (2011). *Urban literacies: Critical perspectives on language, learning, and community.* New York, NY: Teachers College Press.

Lam, W.S.E. (2004). Border discourses and identities in transnational youth culture. In J. Mahiri (Ed.), *What they don't learn in school: Literacy in the lives of urban youth* (pp. 79–98). New York, NY: Peter Lang.

Lam, W.S.E. (2006). Culture and learning in the context of globalization: Research directions. *Review of Research in Education, 30*(1), 213–237.

Lam, W.S.E., & Rosario-Ramos, E. (2009). Multilingual literacies in transnational digitally mediated contexts: An exploratory study of immigrant teens in the United States. *Language and Education, 23*(2), 171–190.

Lam, W.S.E., & Warriner, D. S. (2012). Transnationalism and literacy: Investigating the mobility of people, languages, texts, and practices in contexts of migration. *Reading Research Quarterly, 47*(2), 191–215.

Lee, C. D. (2007). *Culture, literacy and learning: Taking bloom in the midst of the whirlwind.* New York, NY: Teachers College Press.

MacGillivray, L., & Curwen, M. S. (2007). Tagging as a social literacy practice. *Journal of Adolescent and Adult Literacy, 50*(5), 354–369.

Martínez, R. A. (2010). Spanglish as literacy tool: Toward an understanding of the potential role of Spanish-English codeswitching in the development of academic literacy. *Research in the Teaching of English, 45*(2), 124–149.

Martínez-Roldán, C., & Fránquiz, M. E. (2009). Latina/o youth literacies: Hidden funds of knowledge. In L. Christenbury, R. Bomer, & P. Smagorinksy (Eds.), *Handbook of adolescent literacy research* (pp. 323–342). New York, NY: Guilford Press.

Mazzucato, V., & Schans, D. (2011). Transnational families and the well-being of children: Conceptual and methodological challenges. *Journal of Marriage and Family. 73*(4), 704–712.

McCormick, P. (2006). *Sold.* New York, NY: Hyperion Books.

Miles, M. B., & Huberman, M. (1994). *Qualitative data analysis: An expanded sourcebook.* Thousand Oaks, CA: Sage Publications.

Morrell, E. (2002). Toward a critical pedagogy of popular culture: Literacy development among urban youth. *Journal of Adolescent and Adult Literacy, 46*(1), 72–77.

National Center for Educational Statistics. (2013). *Characteristics of public and private elementary and secondary schools in the United States: Results from the 2011–12 schools and staffing survey.* Washington, DC: U.S. Department of Education.

New London Group. (1996). A pedagogy of multiliteracies: Designing social futures, *Harvard Educational Review, 66*(1), 60–92.

Nobles, J. (2011). Parenting from abroad: Migration, nonresident father involvement, and children's education in Mexico. *Journal of Marriage & Family, 73*(4), 729–746.

Oakes, J. (1987). *Tracking in secondary schools: A contextual perspective.* Santa Monica, CA: The Rand Corporation.

Oakes, J. (2005). *Keeping track: How schools structure inequality.* New Haven, CT: Yale University Press.

Orellana, M. F. (2007). Moving words and worlds: Reflections from "the middle." In C. Lewis, P. Enciso, & E. B. Moje (Eds.), *Reframing sociocultural research on literacy: Identity, agency, and power* (pp. 123–136). Mahwah, NJ: Erlbaum.

Orellana, M. F., & Reynolds, J. F. (2008). Cultural modeling: Leveraging bilingual skills for school paraphrasing tasks. *Reading Research Quarterly, 43*(1), 48–65.

Owodally, A.M.A. (2011). Multilingual language and literacy practices and social identities in Sunni madrassahs in Mauritius: A case study. *Reading Research Quarterly, 46*(2), 134–155.

Paris, D. (2011). *Language across difference: Ethnicity, communication, and youth identities in changing urban schools.* Cambridge, England: Cambridge University Press.

Rosaldo, R. (1989). *Culture and truth: The remaking of social analysis.* Boston, MA: Beacon Press.

Rubinstein-Ávila, E. (2007). From the Dominican Republic to Drew High: What counts as literacy for Yanira Lara? *Reading Research Quarterly, 42*(4), 568–589.

Sánchez, P. (2007a). Cultural authenticity and transnational Latina youth: Constructing a meta-narrative across borders. *Linguistics and Education, 18*(3–4), 258–282.

Sánchez, P. (2007b). Urban immigrant students: How transnationalism shapes their world learning. *The Urban Review, 39*(5), 489–517.

Sánchez, P. (2009, April/May). Even beyond the local community: A close look at Latina youth's return trips to Mexico. *The High School Journal 92*(4), 49–66.

Sarroub, L. K. (2002). In-betweenness: Religion and conflicting visions of literacy. *Reading Research Quarterly, 37*(2), 130–148.

Siskin, L. S. (1994). *Realms of knowledge: Academic departments in secondary schools.* Washington, DC: The Falmer Press.

Skerrett, A. (2008). "Going the race way": Biographical influences on multicultural and antiracist English curriculum practices. *Teaching and Teacher Education, 24*, 1813–1826.

Skerrett, A. (2009). Melting pot influences on secondary English curriculum policy. *International Journal of Education Policy & Leadership, 4*(11), 1–12. Available at www.ijepl.org.

Skerrett, A. (2010). Of literary import: A case of cross-national similarities in the secondary English curriculum in the United States and Canada. *Research in the Teaching of English, 45*(1), 36–58.

Skerrett, A. (2011). A case of generativity in a culturally and linguistically complex English language arts classroom. *Changing English: Studies in Culture and Education, 18*(1), 85–97.

Skerrett, A. (2012a). Languages and literacies in translocation: Experiences and perspectives of a transnational youth. *Journal of Literacy Research, 44*(4), 364–395.

Skerrett, A. (2012b). "We hatched in this class": Repositioning of identity in and beyond a reading classroom. *The High School Journal, 95*(3), 62–75.

Skerrett, A. (2013). Building multiliterate and multilingual writing practices and identities. *English Education, 45*(4), 322–360.

Skerrett, A. (2014). Religious literacies in a secular literacy classroom. *Reading Research Quarterly, 49*(2), 233–250.

Skerrett, A., & Bomer, R. (2011.) Borderzones in adolescents' literacy practices: Connecting out-of-school literacies to the reading curriculum. *Urban Education, 46*(6), 1256–1279.

Skerrett, A., & Bomer, R. (2013). Recruiting languages and lifeworlds for border-crossing compositions. *Research in the Teaching of English, 47*(3), 313–337.

Smagorinsky, P. (2008). *Teaching English by design: How to create and carry out instructional units.* Portsmouth, NH: Heinemann.

Sutherland, L. M. (2008). Black adolescent girls' use of literary practices to negotiate boundaries of ascribed identity. *Journal of Literacy Research, 37*(3), 365–406.

Viera, K. (2011). Undocumented in a documentary society: Textual borders and transnational religious literacies. *Written Communication, 28*(4), 436–461.

Wallace, C. (2008). Literacy and identity: A view from the bridge in two multicultural London schools. *Journal of Language, Identity, and Education, 7*(1), 61–80.

Yi, Y. (2008). Relay writing in an adolescent online community. *Journal of Adolescent and Adult Literacy, 51*(8), 670–680.

Young, M.F.D. (1971). An approach to the study of curricula as socially organized knowledge. In M.F.D. Young (Ed.), *Knowledge and control: New directions for the sociology of education* (pp. 19–46). London, England: Collier MacMillan.

Young, V. A. (2007). *Your average nigga: Performing race, literacy, and masculinity.* New York, NY: Teachers College Press.

Zúñiga, V., & Hamann, E. T. (2009). Sojourners in Mexico with U.S. school experience: A new taxonomy for transnational students. *Comparative Education Review, 53*(3), 329–353.

Zúñiga, V., Hamann, E. T., & Sánchez García, J. (2008). *Transnational students: Mexican schools face globalization.* Mexico City, Mexico: Ministry of Education.

Index

About the Author

Allison Skerrett began her English teaching career at Dorchester High School in Boston Public Schools. She is currently an associate professor in the College of Education at The University of Texas at Austin and directs the College's UTeach Urban Teachers secondary English education program. Allison teaches courses such as adolescent literacy and teaching secondary English and reading to preservice and practicing English teachers. Her research explores language and literacy in the lives of diverse youths in outside-school contexts and how English teachers can draw upon students' cultural, linguistic, and multiliteracies repertoires to promote academic development. Allison received the Literacy Research Association's Early Career Achievement Award in 2013. Her research has been published in journals such as *English Education*, *Reading Research Quarterly*, *Research in the Teaching of English*, and *Urban Education*.